GET
IN
THE
GAME

JONATHAN STRINGFIELD

GET IN THE GAME

HOW TO LEVEL UP YOUR BUSINESS
WITH GAMING, ESPORTS, AND EMERGING TECHNOLOGIES

WILEY

For general information on our other products and services or for technical support, please contact our Customer Care Department within the United States at (800) 762-2974, outside the United States at (317) 572-3993 or fax (317) 572-4002.

Wiley publishes in a variety of print and electronic formats and by print-on-demand. Some material included with standard print versions of this book may not be included in e-books or in print-on-demand. If this book refers to media such as a CD or DVD that is not included in the version you purchased, you may download this material at http://booksupport.wiley.com. For more information about Wiley products, visit www.wiley.com.

Library of Congress Cataloging-in-Publication Data is Available:

ISBN 9781119855361 (Hardback)
ISBN 9781119855385 (ePDF)
ISBN 9781119855378 (ePub)

COVER ART & DESIGN: PAUL McCARTHY

SKY10034653_060222

This book is dedicated to my mom, Lee Stringfield, who encouraged my love of gaming and writing throughout my life. I think she would be proud of the result.

Contents

Preface: The Revolution of 1972

The year 1972 not only irrevocably changed the consumer entertainment ecosystem, but also set into motion events that continue to fundamentally alter the ways in which humans interrelate via
media. More specifically, two distinct but related phenomena were
occurring in the world.

First, the Magnavox Odyssey was released, which is widely
considered to be the first home gaming console. The home console shifted the center of gravity for video games from the arcade
to the home. Though the transition period would be tumultuous,
including a crash that nearly capsized the entire industry less than a
decade away, interactive entertainment had found a home in living
rooms across the globe by merit of being an accessory to existing
home technology (it connected to a standard television set) rather
than requiring a separate (and expensive) monitor. In one sense,
1972 is the year that video games shifted from being occasion- and
geographic-bounded entertainment to personal, accessible, and
scaled—attributes that would paint the success of the industry for
decades to come.

Second, beyond the living room and within the venerated halls
of Stanford University, the first digital gaming competition was being
held. A tournament around the early-computer gaming favorite
Spacewar! was being held at the artificial intelligence lab, complete
with multiple competitors and a valuable prize (a yearlong subscrip-
tion to *Rolling Stone*). In a similar parallel to home consoles, this was
the beginning of a tumultuous history, inclusive of a near-existential

industry crash all its own. Thus, in another sense, 1972 is also the year in which the now-global phenomenon of esports was born.

As far as technological and cultural revolutions go (and I'll argue that we'll be addressing a bit of both), 1972 is a pivotal year. The commonality between these events was that interactive entertainment had come to roost (albeit in different legacies reflected in modern times). It also represents a rare opportunity where the occasionally confusing and not always well-documented history of gaming and esports intersect in a meaningful way within a single year. Here we find one of our first major problems when discussing gaming—the industry is multifaceted, expansive, manifest in a number of forms, and carries a long history that speaks to the powerful intersection of technology and creativity.

And yet, to the uninitiated or unaware, you'd never know that was the case. For too long, gaming has been considered a monolithic entity that amounts to little more than the frivolous pastime of children. Fast-forward to today, and the reality is that gaming represents a global, multibillion-dollar ecosystem within which about one in every three humans on the planet is a participant, and is positioned to shape the contours of our relationship with technology for years to come. Despite the scale and influence of this sector, it has become abundantly clear that there is a significant knowledge gap between business decision makers and an industry that, in fairness, has a reputation for being extremely cloistered. Unfortunately, this gap is quickly transitioning from a curiosity to a strategic blind spot for businesses across nearly every industry as the influence of gaming and gaming-related concepts begin to shape technologies as fundamental as the internet.

Character Sheet: Approach and Intended Audience of This Book

For business decision makers and marketers, those who know that gaming is important but haven't yet figured out their point of view, an understanding of the gaming ecosystem and knowing how to integrate with it beyond the superficial is set to become one of the most important tool kits in modern business. While there are many ways a person or organization can enter the expansive gaming ecosystem, understanding and aligning on the right strategic fit, including the proper historical background and a deep understanding of consumer psychology and need states around these media, will define the most successful integrations. In addition, having a perspective on common business concerns related to brand safety and toxicity within the gaming community, including the genesis of these (occasionally overblown) concerns from societal and cultural orientations towards gaming, will balance fact from fiction in evaluating potential opportunities.

Parents seeking to understand what is likely occupying the majority of their children's leisure time may also find value in learning more about the history, landscape, and benefits of gaming in a broader context. Although interest in gaming is not a demarcation between adults and children (given that fans of gaming are not predominately children), there are indeed some generational divides. Despite differences in how one might be exposed to gaming or why one might wish to learn more from a personal or professional standpoint, the most hyperbolic claim I'll make is that nearly everyone stands to gain something from a deeper understanding of gaming as the proliferation of this ecosystem is inevitable. It is massive, big-budget entertainment that lives on an increasing array of devices. It is shaping or creating new economies.

However, gaming is expansive and occasionally confusing—to date, even baseline education (or pitches) for the industry have had limited impact because of how much ground needed to be covered to properly discuss the industry. Most senior officers at businesses have a baseline familiarity (and have very likely used)

Preface: The Revolution of 1972

with a social network or have viewed a television show, but fewer may have kept up with gaming. This book is being written as an important step to creating foundational knowledge upon which better conversations within the industry can be based and better alliances between the gaming sector and interested partners can be formed. It's esoteric at first glance, but not impossible to navigate in a way that clarifies the rather immense industry that has grown behind the scenes of larger cultural attention. More generally, the consumer intention–centric view that will be a central theme throughout this work can serve as a useful rubric for evaluating virtually any new media.

Mini-Map: How This Book Is Structured

This book is divided into roughly three parts to consider different means of ingress into the gaming ecosystem: First, through experiences where consumers are directly *playing* video games, second to occasions and media where consumers are *watching* video games being played. Lastly, we will close by considering future directions for the industry and aligned businesses utilizing the potential emergence of the metaverse as an organizing principle. Each section provides an overview of the history of the platforms, the unique need states that a consumer is satisfying within each mode of entertainment, and addresses throughout substantive topics related to the needs and orientations of three major stakeholders: businesses looking to integrate, game or content developers, and game fans.

I use the term "fan" instead of the more common parlance of "gamer" for a number of reasons. The most obvious is that some of the potential integrations into gaming may have little to do with someone playing a game per se—the intended consumer is watching an esports match or game streamer, etc. On the other hand (and the topic will be addressed more substantively later on), the term "gamer" is incredibly problematic for marketers and business execu-tives to rely on. Even within gaming communities it's a loaded (and, occasionally, negative) term, but above and beyond that it assumes a kind of identity valuation from either the game players themselves or the marketers that want to reach them. Identity is a complicated topic, symbols and labels even more so, and much is to be lost in relying on "shorthand" language of this type when engaging with a commu-nity that prizes authenticity (though we will qualify certain groups of "traditional" game players on occasion, where useful to enunciate a small but significant subset of the larger gaming audience).

The use of the word "fan" also refocuses the discussion on semi-familiar ground. Marketers have generally acknowledged the power of fandom. People "geek out" about a whole host of media, inclusive of mainstays like TV shows or movies. However, the departure here is that we are taking fandom to a new level—fandom that is deeply participatory, shaped by the fans, and highly affective in a way that can only be accomplished when the protagonist is perhaps not a scripted figment of a professional writer's imagination but rather reflects the values and decision of the media consumer. In other words, a world where the fan is the hero of the story, or capable of taking on the same abilities and persona of their favorite athlete. We are through the fourth wall and on the stage.

The emphasis on histories and assessing different vantage points within the industry is a result of the complexities surrounding game development or creating viewership experiences from games. Video games and video game experiences come in a variety of different for-mats, with varying degrees of focus on things like the story, mechan-ics (what is the actual game to be played?), and visual world-building. The single biggest place where brands fail in gaming is overriding any of the core game elements or intended output of a given content producer. Even now as content creators are finding a voice in larger marketing or business decisions, it's important to remember that the intent of the creators is important—particularly when it shapes an experience that encompasses the entirety of a consumer's attention.

As such, one must understand the intent of the gameplay or viewing experience to be successful. An area of focus for this book is to provide the foundational knowledge on games, esports, and related vectors through which a brand or business may wish to integrate. This relies on an understanding of the historical precedent of these industries, along with the motivations fans have towards engagement. In doing so, we'll have a platform for contextualizing key facts about the history of gaming that are less known to those outside the industry or not invested in it. Given that gaming is often at the forefront of technological innovation with consumers, there is much to be learned here, even above and beyond a desire to find a strategic point of entry into the gaming ecosystem.

Finally, the usage of the term "ecosystem" throughout is to clarify that gaming and esports are not monolithic entities, nor are there simply a singular touch point, app, or piece of hardware to consider. Gaming experiences can happen on virtually every screen. They're in the living room and on the subway. There are social portals, communities, content streams, and organized competitive leagues across a truly global audience. While seemingly daunting at first, each subsequent chapter will address a substantive aspect of this ecosystem to yield a more holistic understanding:

Chapter 1 summarizes the current state of gaming and discusses the aim of this book in that context. It examines the different industries and forms involved in gaming, covers key data points about its prevalence, and identifies some of the reasons why broader industry knowledge around gaming has been underdeveloped.

Chapter 2 opens with a history of the rise of gaming, emphasizing the design and monetary aspects that have pushed gaming to ubiquity and in doing so have created the most flexible canvas for integrations with the gaming ecosystem, based upon the simple fact that gaming will be increasingly reliant on these revenue sources to remain sustainable. We'll review this history through a lens that emphasizes cultural, technological, and generational factors that have created the industry that we see today.

In Chapter 3 we'll look to the psychology and motivations behind why people play video games. Much of the appeal of integrations in this space is in reference to the unique way in which video games capture attention; understanding the "why" of this attention is therefore essential. We'll also begin to tackle the concept of what a "gamer" is and how identity is often tightly wrapped up in play due to the participatory nature of gaming media.

In Chapter 4 we'll address concerns around gaming related to brand safety. More specifically, we'll review the facts and fictions around thorny topics such as violence, addiction, and toxicity in gaming cultures using relevant scientific literature and broader discussions around cultural acceptances of new media.

Chapter 5 is the first of two chapters directly related to opportunities for integration, in this case focused on business and marketing integrations within or adjacent to game environments, to engage consumers playing games. Leveraging the background from preceding chapters, we'll evaluate the best mechanisms for integration pending the needs of the business.

Chapter 6 introduces gaming as a viewing experience, beginning with an introduction to the world of esports. The business of esports and game viewing via streaming have a number of parallels to traditional competitive entertainment; nevertheless, esports still exhibit a number of important differentiators related to changing tastes in video consumption.

Chapter 7 addresses the history of esports, if only to dispel the notion that esports are an "overnight" fad. The chapter also highlights the important social, technological, and cultural movements that created the global phenomenon as we understand it today.

Chapter 8 opens up the discussion of viewing to streaming more generally; here we will dive into the typologies of streaming content, their numerous interactions with both the esports and generalized gaming ecosystems, and the unique pressures that arise from the overlap of "work" and "play."

Chapter 9 concludes our discussion on opportunities present in viewing game content, by outlining opportunities for integration in esports and generalized gaming streaming. As with the previous chapter on integration opportunities within gaming, we'll leverage the background provided by preceding chapters to outline strategies most primed for success.

Chapter 10 adopts a future-looking view on forthcoming opportunities in gaming and esports. Potentially influential technologies and trends, broadly related to the emergence of the metaverse, will be outlined as a guide towards what decision makers should keep their eyes on after they have established a solid foundation in gaming more generally from the preceding chapters.

Chapter 11 is our concluding chapter, where we'll summarize the most important trends outlined throughout as a means to orient toward broader ramifications that gaming and game viewing entail for the future of communicating with consumers, if not technology more generally.

It's this approach, I believe, that is the best path to understanding the large, occasionally complicated, but undoubtedly valuable world of gaming—both as a means to understand and leverage current opportunities, but also to provide a strategic foundation for the future forms that gaming and gaming-related opportunities will take.

A few final caveats before we begin in earnest: First, any worthwhile work addressing new or changing media recognizes that you're essentially chasing a moving target. Technology changes and preferences are fickle—what was a popular game or platform today very well may not be tomorrow. As a result, we will not be focusing on the minute details, formats, or avenues for integration so much as discussing overarching strategies with nods toward tactical themes or examples where useful.

Second, although at the time of this writing I hold an executive position at a very large gaming publisher, this book contains no specialized knowledge, nor is it intended as a long marketing proposition for any given game organization. For practical (and contractual) purposes, that isn't the point—even in my official capacity I'm quick to point out that my job isn't to extol the virtues of any one publisher. The non-gaming industry isn't completely ready for that—we're still wrapping our head around gaming more generally, and this book is written out of recognition of that problem and to contribute to a (to date) nascent body of work that can up-level understandings of gaming more generally, and the necessary precursors for businesses and marketers to be successful in these important worlds. I approach this work as an academic social scientist whose research has often focused on how individuals integrate new technologies in their lives, a business and technology executive who works with brands to understand new technologies, and an expert in the domain of gaming more generally (from both personal and professional practice—as you might suspect, I'm a lifelong gaming fan).

Finally, just by writing this book I'm risking the scorn of the community that I'm helping others understand. For those of you with some degree of familiarity with this space—that is, my fellow enthusiasts, who are often endlessly and ruthlessly cynical—a book like this (a business book, no less!) augurs a dark future of freemium shovelwear, lousy game experiences, and corporate interests overriding the wholly unique blend of technological innovation, creativity, and story telling that makes gaming special. The easy take is that this book, and my intentions, are yet another strike to the heart of something you hold dear.

I want you to understand that this shift is already happening. Where the eyeballs and engagement are, so goes the money. It's only a matter of time; this can be a positive or negative influence, and this book is designed to provide the necessary framework for these influences to be positive. On a personal note, gaming has framed a lot of my life, and I want it to thrive and be healthy and influential to others. In this light, I don't want to sneak outside interests in through the back door. I'd prefer to usher them in the front door, but only after taking their shoes off first. So, to my fellow fans—I wrote this book because I love gaming. Passion drove this book, passion drives the gaming community, and authenticity always wins.

To my colleagues in the business word who are not yet fans (and may never be), I wrote this book because I believe that business leaders who respect this passion and speak with authenticity can be a positive influence in this space, and they can reach consumers in one of the most affective and transformative platforms in existence. I believe that we are approaching a time when the skills and foundational understanding of gaming will not be optional, but essential—not simply for near-term opportunities but also for the future of media that will be manifested via practices and technologies that gaming pioneered.

Part I

Playing the Game: Understanding Video Games as Media

Chapter 1

Introduction

The Gaming Moment

Outnumbered and depleted of resources, I slam my shield into a ghostly guardsman of Shadowfang Keep, hoping to knock him off the rhythm of blows that have been raining down on my head.

"I need some help."

An arrow whizzes by to my right, though it lands not against the group of foes I'm currently facing but squarely into a second patrol of guardsmen who had not yet reached our location. An error, and potentially a costly one. Alerted to our presence, the guards run to join the fray and add to the already insurmountable odds in front of our stalwart group of five heroes, aiming to free the keep from its foul master, Archmage Arugal.

"*We* need *a lot* of help," I say, soliciting any ideas from the team to turn around a seemingly hopeless situation.

"I got it, Dad."

A surge of light fills the air as a healing spell cast by our team priest mends our wounds. Reinvigorated, the remainder of our front line presses the attack, systematically striking down the undead guardsmen.

"Nice job, Heals, sorry about the extra pull," our companion Hunter and originator of the stray arrow whispers to the rest of the party. "This is a great group, much better coordination than most randos."

"Thanks," I write back, "probably because most of us are all in the same room."

Our team was indeed *not* mostly comprised of "randos" (a random assortment of players)—I filled the team role of "Tank" (protector of the group), supported by my wife as "DPS" (damage-dealer) and teenage son as "Heals" (keeping the rest of the team healthy and alive). We arranged a collection of laptops and PCs together in our suburban home, seeking adventure and daring with wild abandon of our virtual safety in the expansive *World of Warcraft* as an escape from the very real dangers outside our home during the height of the COVID-19 pandemic.

While the settings of this particular adventure were catalyzed by the rather extreme circumstances of a global pandemic, the more basic phenomenon at play here is not new to our family nor to many families like us around the world—parents who are increasingly using gaming as a means to connect with their children. And perhaps more important, games feature prominently in the everyday entertainment of individuals of varying ages, backgrounds, and needs across the world.

The impact of the COVID-19 pandemic is reflected not only in the body of this work (as the historical moment within which it was written), but also stands as a particularly meaningful moment in media and culture when gaming was thrust into the spotlight of popular attention. The last few years have become one of the most important moments for the reception and understanding of gaming within popular culture. Make no mistake, gaming had been steadily on the rise for years and decades before, but with the reassembly of meaning of our everyday lives comes the reassessment of the ways in which we consume media. Put another way, the influence of COVID-19 on gaming was less a catalyst and more a lens through which a broader group of consumers and decision makers across the world saw the impact of gaming on everyday lives. The household scenario described above has been played out in innumerable homes across the world.

Dads, moms, millennials, Gen Z, financial advisors, lawyers, and others from all walks of life are among the billions of consumers logging innumerable hours across a multitude of purpose-built and generalized consumer devices across one of the largest and rapidly growing media ecosystems in the world—video gaming. Often misunderstood, seldom discussed beyond the semicloistered businesses that support it and fandom that fuels it, recent circumstances have shined the spotlight on video gaming, not just as a participatory media, but as a professionalized pursuit (esports).

When focusing on the professional side of gaming, I found it instructive to travel across the world from my home in metro New York to Tokyo for another example. Portions of this book were written during the 2020 Summer Olympics in Tokyo. Any Olympics has a heavy impact on popular culture, but these particular games are noteworthy in a book about gaming for a number of reasons—first, Tokyo is the mecca of video gaming, and its influence on the games was portrayed throughout the games: From Japanese, Prime Minister Shinzo Abe dressed as Super Mario for the countdown to Tokyo's Summer Games, to upwards of 19 video game scores, ranging from *Final Fantasy* to *Sonic the Hedgehog*, being played during the parade of nations (yes, really).

Second, the most apparent abnormality in the 2020 Olympiad was the fact that some of the most hallowed and long-standing traditions in sports were left without an audience. Sport as we know it had faced innumerable disruptions over the previous year (including the fact that the "2020" Summer Games were held in 2021). In fact, seasons for many sports were canceled because they require physical contact. In other cases, competitions were held in empty arenas.

Throughout this time of disruption, one type of competitive entertainment could still be played at the highest levels—esports.

While the artifacts and conduct of esports couldn't fully escape the impact of COVID-19 (even games played virtually require massive amounts of technological coordination to ensure that the virtual playing field remains fair), here too emerged a moment where the superpowers of gaming and esports became profoundly clear—both are media that don't require physical contact for socialization or competition.

As one looked upon the empty stands in Tokyo, fundamental questions around the role of audiences and professional competition were posed, especially how the future and definition of sport are changing with the ebbs and flows of technology and culture. Indeed, the International Olympic Committee has been debating the inclusion of esports as a medaled event for a number of years, and we may see this come to fruition as soon at the 2028 Summer Games in Los Angeles. Prior to the traditional Olympic Games, Tokyo hosted the Virtual Olympic Series, a stepping-stone where virtual representations of physical sports (motorsport, cycling, baseball, etc.) were played by an emerging subset of professional competitors.

I don't highlight these examples to overplay the importance of the events of 2020 and 2021 on video games and esports. While the circumstances of those years facilitated an increase in the number of individuals looking for new means of entertainment (creating the occasional new passion or re-investigation of a previous hobby), it did not change the trajectory of these industries so much as give them a boost. What changed was the extent to which the discussion of these forms of media shifted from the periphery to the center of culture. More simply, seemingly everyone came to terms with the fact that gaming was a "thing," and it was having a moment—a moment that has seemingly evolved into a movement.

Late in 2021 the business and technology world became enamored with possibilities of a new, decentralized version of the internet colloquially referred to as Web 3.0. The circumstances of the global pandemic, paired with ongoing interest around the possibilities afforded by blockchain technology, provided fertile ground for concepts such as the metaverse (a persistent, embodied, virtual world that users would traverse as means of accessing this new internet) to take hold. As we will learn, video games have a long history of impacting the ways in which we contextualize new technologies and means of interaction. The isolation imposed by a global pandemic shaped our collective thinking around the possibilities provided by virtual worlds, and virtual worlds have a history dating back almost 50 years in video gaming. Understanding video games has quickly evolved from just a savvy business practice to an essential skill set for maintaining relevancy in the future technology landscape.

These moments and movements speak to broad shifts in consumer behaviors, and from the get-go it's important to clarify that the purpose of this book is not to construct hyperbolic promises around flashes in the pan or buzzy media phenomena that will fade almost as quickly as they came to rise. When we speak about the gaming industry as it exists today we must understand that we are talking about nothing less than a fundamental reorientation around the intersection of technology, culture, fandom, and business. This "gaming moment" very likely brought you to the pages of this book (and in no small way, as we'll discuss, necessitated the creation of this book), and while I promise not to become too deeply academic, what you'll come to understand is that gaming is not just a "new" frontier for savvy marketers and business decision makers. It's a map of how consumers participate in not just the creation of media, but also in the consumption and integration of these multifaceted relationships between consumers, fans, and media. Our understanding of these developments will be greatly enriched and go far beyond a superficial roadmap of tactics.

Understanding the job in front of us, and returning to Shadowfang Keep for a moment, we were soon off to our next adventure.

For those of you wishing to join us in spirit—to understand what will be one of the most essential and fundamental forms of consumer entertainment over the next few decades—allow me to lend you my shield.

Why Gaming Matters, Why Now . . . and Why This Book?

If all of this sounds like a different world from what you're accustomed to . . . well, you're not wrong. But, it's more about different worlds—ones that aren't relegated to the stereotypical basement or archaic arcades. They are sprawling touch points with narratives on par or better than what one can experience on the silver screen, and they're expanding at astonishing rates. Despite this, attention to gaming for industry outsiders remains remarkably low. The divide between where an increasingly diverse base of consumers are spending their time, and where marketers and business decision makers are spending their efforts, are as lopsided today as they were in the early days of social media relative to TV/print advertising.

The precedent is worthwhile to note. The emergence of social media and other user-generated content that typified Web 2.0 required a dramatic realignment among marketers and business decision makers. Legacy web practices such as static banner ads or marketing practices like TV commercials were challenged by digital platforms where businesses were expected to be in dialogue with their consumers, rather than merely directing messages at them. We now stand at the beginning stages of another fundamental shift in the relationships between businesses and consumers in the form of Web 3.0, which hinges in part on traversing virtual worlds, and yet knowledge among businesses on how to orient themselves and integrate within these worlds (and how consumers think about or immerse themselves in them) is only nascent. Gaming has become top of mind for business decision makers because the audience of gaming fans amounts to billions, but it's less well recognized that virtual worlds have been the domain of gaming and gaming fans since nearly the advent of video games, and as such are among the best avenues for orienting business decision makers to this potential future internet.[1]

And yet, video gaming has, both as a consumer pursuit and a business, operated somewhat under the radar of popular culture, and therefore occasionally outside the consideration space of those most entrusted with keeping abreast of popular culture or the means to relate to consumers. The reception to gaming is dramatically different from that at the emergence of social media. Doors at media agencies are not quite opening as readily, and objections to strategies in the space are consistent and incorrect: Gaming is niche (it's not), just for kids (it isn't), or only fit for directly gaming-related partnerships (already well disproven). Specifically, the gaming industry is expected to generate $175 billion in revenue in 2021,[2] compared to the peak box office draw in 2019 of almost $40 billion[3] or $21.6 billion[4] in 2020 for the recorded music industry. Multiple sources estimate the total population of video game players to be in excess of 3 billion people (or at least 40 percent of the global population), including 227 million in the United States alone, where the average age of the player is 31 years, 45 percent identify as female, and 74 percent of households have at least one person who plays video games.[5]

Despite the scale and footprint of the industry, the opportunity within gaming as it stands now is not well known or established in central business practices, even though many decision makers seek to chase the "next big thing," whether it be the metaverse or concepts related to digital ownership. Yet they don't have the foundational knowledge that gaming readily provides.

Reconciling the rise of video gaming amounts to reorienting around fundamental shifts in the consumer media landscape.

Millennials are increasingly becoming household heads and have tastes and preferences for media content and formats that are profoundly different from those of the generations that preceded them. Entire generations of consumers have been playing games their entire lives. They are sharing this passion with their children. They view gaming as interchangeable with watching TV or a movie after work. The attention and passion are there . . . but major brands and partnering companies are not. At least, not yet.

So, to answer the questions we began with are: Why gaming? Why now? Why this book?

Why Gaming?

It is an inevitability in the burgeoning entertainment ecosystem. It is mainstream, blockbuster-level entertainment. Gaming represents the end game of several powerful phenomena in the larger media world, ranging from the impact of participatory media to establishing spatial presence in media. We'll spend time unpacking occasionally esoteric phenomena in media studies and psychology in order to convey the larger point that the rise of gaming portends more fundamental shifts in the relationship between consumers and media, and therefore the means and practices through which a marketer or business decision maker should relay a message. Gaming matters because it's not simply an app or new platform; it's a way of relating to media in a more general sense, and it's a way of relating to media that is becoming increasingly influential in a wider array of contexts, inclusive of those seminal to whatever form Web 3.0 may take.

Why Now?

Certainly one can point to the acceleration of gaming conversations around the global pandemic or enthusiasm around the metaverse, but realistically the business world has already been long overdue for a reckoning with gaming. We are quickly approaching a tipping point where mastery of concepts around gaming are no longer merely "nice to have" but have become an essential tool for virtually any business. It's not too late to get in front of this shift, but time is running scarce.

Why This Book?

Well, the simple truth is because of the sum of the factors noted above, it needs to exist. To be blunt, the larger business community is, in some respects, behind, and calcified around misconceptions that are impeding meaningful learning and education. Baseline references on this phenomenon are sadly lacking—this is due in no small part to the historical precedent of gaming sitting on the periphery of popular culture (and the entertainment business industry). However, without some fundamental knowledge we will not be able to progress towards the quality and depth of conversations that should be occurring around this now massive industry. Moreover, because the connection that this type of media has with its fandom is unique and deeply affective, the potential for missteps is quite high, yet easily avoidable.

And while several books exist on gaming, esports, or streaming, few consider the ecosystem around gaming more generally. Fewer still address these industries beyond the superficial, or how businesses outside of gaming should view and integrate this industry. I've found that decision makers may not be able to distinguish a game from an esport or understand how streaming and esports are related, or why video games are increasingly not only the domain of gaming consoles.

In short, it's not just time, we're overdue, but I'm hoping this work can "power level" your understanding appropriately (we'll chip away at some of the gaming jargon, too).

Chapter 2

Tricks Your TV Can Do

The Rise, Fall, and Rise Again of Gaming

Any history of video games comes across the same problem: "Video games" as a concept are somewhat ill defined, and even accepting some of the more agreed-upon features of the definition, one is still faced with a history that is not linear nor easy to follow. Such a history is a mess of starts and stops, influences that pop up within a given period but are not fully developed for some years later, and various technological or cultural shifts in society. Moreover, like any technology, its trajectory is moving forward and shifting even as these very words are written—most technology histories are out of date by the time they go to press.

So, why bother? Put simply, the truth is that much of the logic of the current state of gaming can be rationalized by understanding its origins. It is also the case that gaming has long held a particular role in the overall history of consumer technology, where it has been a reference point for contextualizing and understanding new technologies. Video games were a mechanism through which coin-operated machines were sanitized for "respectable" household consumption, televisions were adapted from being purely "passive" mediums of engagement, and cellular phones could showcase functionality beyond merely making calls. Games have a long history of being "tricks" that other technology could perform, and therefore have a shared history with some of the most fundamental corners of the consumer technology landscape. For marketers reading this book, it is with some irony that video games have become one of the biggest yet least understood opportunities, and yet gaming found a foothold in the home by alleviating certain concerns around the platform par excellence of advertising, television.[1]

However, it is easy (and incorrect) to assume that the adoption of gaming has simply been a question of technology. Through the relatively short history of video games there have been ebbs and flows of design around game systems that required more specialized knowledge and dedicated time to play versus quicker experiences with simplified controls allowing for broader adoption. Games became a seemingly niche activity designed for a narrow demographic of players for a period of time that occupies only a few decades of its history, but has shaped perceptions of gaming in the United States even today.

This is in part due to the fact that games are first and foremost a consumer entertainment product. Though there are immense implications for a variety of industries and social practices in the future (in addition to the innumerable opportunities present today), the history of games is one of conforming to the economic realities of a business coming to grips with societies that would view them with suspicion given their relatively recent nature. What was once a business model optimized for young men has become significantly broader as the early economic models gaming was built around have become unsustainable as the result of the increasing costs and complexity of modern game design.

The history of games most useful for our purposes here is about how we thread technology, and later games, into our everyday life. Gaming is reaching critical mass and touching more consumers than ever by merit of how it has adapted to being interwoven into daily life. This is, in some respects, a return to design sensibilities that trace back to the beginning of video games. As such, the history that we will

14

review is less an exhaustive accounting of various consoles, games, or IP, but rather the lineage of important trends in modern gaming tracing back to its earliest days where it has evolved from a series of "tricks" new technology can do to a broad spectrum of entertainment that is accessible and applicable to nearly everyone. We'll approach this history in a mostly linear fashion in terms of chronology (though at times we'll describe periods with some overlap, when notable but disparate developments were occurring around the same time, such as the early 1990s) but focus on broader themes that have set the stage for the modern era of gaming, which stands to be one where gaming has emerged at the center of popular culture.

We can trace these patterns of the rise of gaming through roughly five eras, each demarcated by important shifts in the economic, social, or technological landscape that influenced the world of gaming as it exists today:

The Big Computer Era (~1962–1971): The earliest days of video games were limited to research institutions, given their unique access to computer technology. The advent of computer technology came hand in hand with gaming, as games were used as a demonstration of the technology at the time, though one that had limited availability and interest beyond those in large research institutions.

Coin Drops and Consoles Era (~1972–1984): Much of this changed with *Pong*. For a time, video games were postured as a more socially acceptable form of the coin-slot game, shedding the unsavory origins of these machines in unruly parlors designed for gambling to the family-friendly consumer mecca of the suburban shopping mall. However, *Pong* emerged as the first truly commercially viable game, leading to a proliferation of arcades and home consoles marketed as fun for the whole family.

The Console and Culture Wars (~1985–1993): Low quality and confusing choices led to a collapse of the game industry in the early 1980s, tapering broader consumer excitement around the medium aside from the young men for whom those games were largely designed and marketed. New market entrants corrected the underlying cause of the crash by merit of tighter quality controls, while many (if not all) of the social and cultural biases towards gaming were cemented during this period, epitomized by congressional hearings over the impact of gaming on youth in the United States.

The PC and Mobile Era (~1990–2005): Though home video game console technology continued to develop into increasingly sophisticated machines, the most significant developments that led to the proliferation of gaming were the result of broad consumer adoption of personal computers, domestic internet, and mobile phones. PC gaming found new life in networked play, while games on phones set the stage for one of the more fundamental technological revolutions for the industry. Just as significantly, game design that broadened focus beyond idealized "gamers" of the previous era were becoming more common, in tandem with the "blockbuster" model of game development, which necessitated this expanded focus in game design.

The Casual Revolution (~2006–Now): The modern era of gaming is defined by flexible and easily understandable mimetic interfaces, wide technological access of quality games via smartphones and regulated app marketplaces, and games designed for everyone. It is, in short, an era differentiated by games that are no longer simply "tricks" for new technology nor reliant on specialized knowledge held by a closed demographic of dedicated game players, but a fundamental shift in technology, design, and economics of games towards a model in which nearly every consumer can touch the larger ecosystem in a way that makes sense for them.

Notably, the history as described here is designed to disabuse us of the notion that there is one definitive technology or shift that catapulted gaming to the near ubiquity it enjoys today. We tend to think about the rise of gaming in recent years as the sole output of smartphones, where the phase "everyone has a game console in their pocket" is oft referenced. While this is true in some respects, it only tells part of the story. Any given game console (pocketable or not) is only as good as the games on it, and it is impossible to introduce millions to the world of gaming without games that appeal to them. The rise of gaming was unlocked by accessible technology, but it was driven by an economic imperative to design games for a larger potential fandom and to find mechanisms to finance games differentially from the model that had been the basis of game sales for decades (returning, in some respects to some of the earliest models of game play transactions).

Games massified to the scale of media because they had to—simply put, the economic models of early game development were not sustainable given modern market realities. This necessitated appealing to a broader demographic though flexible economics and network effects, yielding profitable and recurrent revenue streams. The inevitable rise of gaming is based upon cultural acceptance, but that acceptance is predicated on understanding, and understanding only truly comes from contact. The economic necessity for games to shift their focus to a larger fan base had the additional effect of normalizing video games in both the West and the East.

Even as we trace a history where gaming has risen and fallen, for games to once again to slip back to the periphery of culture seems like an impossibility given their prevalence today. Due in part to the unique way gaming has evolved, the genie has been let out of the bottle. To understand why, we must understand the cultural, economic, and societal circumstances leading to this point.

The Big Computer Era (~1962–1971)

Before big data we had big computers. Real big. Room-sized. Each representing monumental steps forward in human development, unlocking new worlds of mathematics, physics, interstellar travel, and our capability to ingest and make sense of unfathomable amounts of data. Naturally, we wanted to play with them as well.

While the earliest record of a game played through a computer interface could likely be traced to the "Nimrod Digital Computer" (intuitively enough, designed to play the mathematical game "nim") for the 1951 Festival of Britain,[2] the first that employed cathode ray screens (thereby putting the "video" in video games) can be attributed to early computers relegated to research labs, universities, and government facilities in the late 1950s and early 1960s. One of the earliest games to utilize a screen, *Tennis for Two*, was designed by American physicist William Higinbotham in 1958 for a public exhibition at the Brookhaven National Laboratory.[3] The computational properties of the massive Donner Model 30 computer were shown off with reference to tennis, a game that nearly everyone knew something about. In this sense, the earliest computers were made relatable by means of games that could be played on the technology—a common use case for games, which reoccurs up to and beyond the point of smartphones.

Since the earliest computers, designing games has been part of the culture of technological mastery surrounding amateur and professional computer programming. During this particular point in the history of computers, such games were primarily limited by the incredibly small install-base of computer machines. *Spacewar!* was a game designed for, and playable on, any given PDP-1 computer, though there numbered only 55 such machines in the world. Even among a paltry number of users, *Spacewar!* is an example of one of the first "distributed" games, in addition to being (as we'll discuss in future chapters) the platform upon which the first esports tournament was held.

While access to the technology was certainly an impediment to wider adoption of the games of this era, they also happened to be exceedingly difficult to play. Games of *Spacewar!* have been likened to attempting to pilot an actual space shuttle, requiring a fairly advanced knowledge of the game mechanics and input interfaces. While this high intellectual barrier was likely one of the more attractive properties of the game for research scientists, it was a non-negligible blocker for the less technologically inclined. Though I would not go so far as to describe these scientists and academics as the first true "hardcore" gamers, who privileged skill and technical mastery of a game system, one should take note of the emerging pattern between specialized knowledge required to play a game versus more intuitive design and interfaces.

To this end, the first break-out hit for video games was a revolution not simply because access to it was freed from massive research facilities, but because it was exceedingly intuitive to play and (once again) rooted in existing cultural knowledge of existing gameplay. What many misattribute as the first video game is in actuality the first broadly, commercially viable game: *Pong*.

Coin-Drops and Consoles Era (~1972–1984)

As far as instructions for games go, you can't get much simpler than what was emblazoned on the first *Pong* cabinets: "Avoid missing the ball for a high score." So simple, it would turn out, one could understand and enjoy the game while pretty drunk. *Pong* debuted at Andy Capp's Tavern in Sunnyvale, California, only to break down after a single evening of game play—not because any particular quirk with the hardware or software, but because the machine overloaded with quarters after a full evening of play.

This enthusiastic (and lucrative) adoption was just what the coin-operated amusements industry needed at the time. Such machines were, for a long time, mostly at home in pretty seedy places. A landmark ruling in 1956 distinguished between games of chance and flipper games like pinball, paving the way for broader acceptance, though never truly shedding associations with gambling and low-brow culture from the 1930s.[4] Video arcades presented a more sanitized, technologically advanced version of coin-operated amusements, fit for the emerging middle class in America. Such arcades soon found homes in malls and other social and commercial centerpieces of society. The sheen of new technology provided acceptability and respectability to a historical business model. Arcade games also happened to be more lucrative than pinball machines and other mainstays, given that they were designed to limit play into relatively quick bursts for all but the most skillful players, thereby requiring another quarter. Or, in the case of Japan, 100-yen coins.

In major Asian markets like Japan, China, and Korea, gaming found welcome homes in shared game spaces such as arcades, even above and beyond those in the United States. Higher levels of social acceptability around video games in Asia (with some important caveats we will note momentarily) have long situated them as acceptable public activities, with proportionally higher quantities of public gaming spaces (relative to the United States) remaining even in more recent times. The acceptability of gaming in Japan is due in part to the fact that some of the earliest innovators in video game development were of Japanese origin, including the developer Taito, which released *Space Invaders* in 1978. Arguably one of the most well-known games of all time, it can also be argued that it is basically an unwinnable game—the alien invaders eventually reach such a speed that failure is all but inevitable. Adoption of this game was so strong that there are disputed accounts of Japan facing shortages of 100-yen coins shortly after its debut in 1978, caused in part by the sheer quantity of the coins being dropped into the machines.[5] Arcade gaming during this period was defined by intuitive but incredibly difficult game play motivated by recorded high scores that sets a hierarchy among players (even those not present in the arcade at time), thereby encouraging thousands of fans to continue to spend money playing. Arcades provided an environment for video games that was both social and competitive, but the prospect of youths wasting away their allowances—in addition to wanting to foster family togetherness—created a market (certainly inclusive of concerned parents) to bring this experience out of the public and into the private.

The first home gaming console, the Magnavox Odyssey, was released in 1972. By today's standards it was a simple affair—the graphics output to the screen were simplistic black and white pixels, and the console included overlays to cling to the screen to bring game environments to life. It also used physical objects like dice, given that this system was broadly conceptualized as a bridge between traditional board games and ones that were technologically facilitated. The proliferation of game consoles at the time, including notable entrants such as Atari and Coleco, were a welcome outlet for interest in gaming that had been built up in arcades but also, as noted above, as a means to assert control over the television.

21

Given the honored place that TVs occupy, literally and figuratively at the center of the household, it is easy to forget that some time ago they were new technology, and not one that was universally accepted. Early criticisms lamented the passive nature of the medium, given how messaging from major broadcasters was forced upon viewers without their having much of a say in what kind of information they would receive (a fear that was partially reinforced by Cold War paranoia around the rise of political ideals imposed by the media).[6] Video game consoles afforded an active, participatory "trick" people could perform on their television set—games weren't just an accessory, but rather a partial antidote to the worst ills of the technology.[7]

It is through this seemingly unlikely path that games became domestic, though only in certain homes. Much like the sanitized sensibility of mall arcades designed for suburban life, game consoles were in fact a largely suburban and affluent pastime: video game consoles were not easily affordable technologies, and ones that are easily enough rationalized as a luxury. Access to gaming, in some respects, has always had divisions around those that could afford more specialized technology versus those that could not. As we'll learn, this is a historical artifact that resonates today in the division of certain esports (notably with the "Fighting Game" community) and broader cultural patterns of game adoption globally.

Though these technologies were originally marketed to appeal to the classic suburban family, in practice early studies of gaming in the domestic sphere found that it was fathers and sons who played together, and thereafter largely the sons once fathers lost interest (partially due to being bested by their children).[8] By the 1980s it was broadly known within the video game industry that the vast majority of its players were young men,[9] thereby intensely focusing not only marketing activities on this demographic, but also game design sensibilities and themes. War, exploration, and sci-fi became the recurrent themes of game environments. Within about a decade from the release of *Pong*, virtually all advertising for video games focused on teenage boys.[10]

However, even in the early stages of gaming there was recognition that there were opportunities beyond this group of young men who would go on to be the primary focus and consumers of the industry through the 1990s. *Pac-Man* (and the curvaceous double-down on the female demographic, *Ms. Pac-Man*) represents a deliberate effort towards more inclusive themes in gaming beyond war and space, albeit from somewhat misplaced good intentions. Toru Iwatani, the designer of *Pac-Man*, designed the game to have a "feminine draw" but focused on things women like, including fashion, dating, or food (with only "eating food" being an interest that could be easily gamified).[11] Even among the earliest examples of extending the reach of gaming beyond young men, one of the fundamental constraints was the exclusively male vantage point of those producing them.

Notable exceptions such as *Pac-Man* aside, teenage boys had commanded the attention of the video games industry. As game consoles found purchase in more homes, these young men sought spaces in the household to explore technologies, including the stereotypical basement complete with accoutrements to play the newly released game system *Dungeons and Dragons* (D&D) in 1974. The storytelling-dependent nature of D&D would influence early game designers for decades, as they computerized tedious parts of the experience such as maps and character sheets—eventually paving the way for Multi-User Dungeon computer games (MUDs), the precursors to role playing and other narrative-intensive arcs in game development (and, arguably, the first manifestation of shared virtual worlds in gaming, meaning that the basis of seemingly new concepts such as the metaverse can be traced back some 50 years).

The communal nature and fantastical themes found in D&D set off a panic among concerned adults in the 1980s[12] that video games would emulate almost a decade later. What occupies disproportionate attention among youths is soon scrutinized among well-meaning parents. Lack of familiarity breeds disproportionate responses that have created starts and stops in broader acceptance of media like video games across different cultures. This era represents one of the most significant ones for gaming not only because many influences in game design and technology can be traced to this period, but because broad commercialization opened a path for wide social acceptance and scrutiny. However, this same path faced a significant detour on the back of an industry crash.

The Console and Culture Wars (~1985–1993)

With any rise there follows the risk of a fall. A crash in the home console market in 1983 is attributable to a number of factors, though it can largely be characterized by a deluge of both home consoles and associated software of poor quality that significantly dampened broader enthusiasm for video games.[13] Teenage boys became not just the focus for the wounded industry, but a lifeline, as their interest in games were not particularly influenced by broader economic concerns.

As a result, what is arguably the most influential home console of all time, the Nintendo Entertainment System (NES), was largely viewed as yet another passing fad by both adults and retailers.[14] Despite considerable barriers, the NES entered the market successfully by tightly controlling supply, enforcing an exacting standard of quality on both their platform and software ("certified" by the now legendary "Nintendo Seal of Approval"), and savvy mass marketing via fanzines (Nintendo Power) and tip lines. Long and short, Nintendo cut a path that was significantly differentiated from the competition with a focus on quality and customer experience. The trajectory for Nintendo, and arguably the entire video game industry, was irrevocably altered as new life was breathed into the ecosystem.

However, success breeds competition. Game aficionados and people indulging in nostalgia will remember the late 1980s and early 1990s as a time defined by a brawl between then-gaming giants Nintendo and Sega over the future of the living room, each engaging in savage marketing and technological blows to win over gaming consumers in a so-called Console War.[15] Young men quickly drew allegiances between the camps of Mario and Sonic, the iconic mascots of Nintendo and Sega, respectively. What it meant to be a "gamer," and have personal identity tied tightly to a pastime and personal purchase, can in part be attributed to the divisive marketing tactics at the time. Even as Sega faded from console products to be replaced by Sony and Microsoft, allegiances to technological console "camps" became a central (and as we'll discuss further, potentially toxic) hallmark of what it meant to be a video game enthusiast.

The marketing push at the time was not in a direction to make games more accessible, but rather to double-down on the perceived needs of young, male gamers—more advanced technology, faster game play, cutting edge visuals. Not only did video gaming find new life during this time, it also molded a subset of consumers that would go on to define the hobby for decades to come. Much of how we view gaming even today is in light of this (comparatively) narrow window in the history of gaming, where it was largely the pursuit of young men outside the bounds of dominant culture. This includes the specialized knowledge required for mastery of a game, and the relative difficulty of the game systems. Games became increasingly complex and esoteric as design philosophies moved from one optimized for anyone to play for a short period of time (or as long as they may like, assuming a large enough roll of quarters) to games for gamers.

The gamer identity is the root of many of the misconceptions around gaming, yet it represents a very real and occasionally problematic fandom that must be contended with (which we'll discuss in depth in subsequent chapters on the psychology of gaming, and issues of toxicity and representation). The combination of young men, with games increasingly relying on tropes of violence and sexuality to motivate sales, catalyzed a series of congressional hearings[16] in 1993 around the influence of violence and other problematic themes in video games on the youth of the United States. Like D&D a decade before, video gaming had found its moment of scrutiny by adults concerned with the impact of an emerging medium on young minds.

Here too, the ramifications of these hearings and the association between gaming and violence are topics we'll address shortly. From a historically oriented perspective, this is a period when video games as a medium matured, and in doing so developed a series of standards and conventions along with a narrowly defined fan base that alienated many players.[17] The emergence of networked personal computers and wide availability of portable phones represents a moment in which this trend of alienation began to reverse, and set the stage for the dualities in modern gaming we see today-dualities that share a common theme of an increased necessity to be interwoven into daily life.

The PC and Mobile Era (~1990–2005)

Since their reemergence in the early 1980s, home consoles have become a mainstay in many households. Despite, at times, pushing the envelope of computational technology, even after multiple releases the framing that video game consoles are for kids has only recently been disrupted by modern iterations that serve as advanced media centers (and a generation of now-adult household decision makers who kept up their interest in gaming, which had been seeded in their childhoods). However, some of the biggest developments for gaming from the perspective of cultural and social acceptability were shaped by personal computers and mobile phones, though the influence of consoles on games across these platforms is significant.

For example, from a more global perspective, the importance of PCs and phones for gaming is in part a direct reflection of the reception of game consoles. Such devices had never found a deep market in China, largely due to the expense of the devices, though a more tangible barrier came in the form of a ban of video game consoles in 2000 (only to be lifted some 14 years later).[18] Similarly, cultural tensions between Japan and Korea structured an Asian market that consolidated around shared game spaces that rapidly incorporated networked PCs (à la Korean PC Bangs or PC Rooms, which we'll explore more in the history of esports) as the de facto platform for gaming. Even in modern times, PCs and mobile phones remain the dominant platforms in both China and Korea, leaving Japan as the only major Asian market with a proportionately significant console footprint.

Stateside, console games like *Super Mario Brothers 3* served as the inspiration to bring smoother game experiences to PC gaming, which were initially limited by short-term memory storage on machines that were ostensibly not designed to be gaming devices. Nothing short of engineering marvels ultimately led to what is arguably the most significant PC game of all time—id Software's *DOOM*.[19] Leading up to and through the release of *DOOM*, id pioneered or mastered a number of important milestones for PC gaming—advanced networking play (where opponents could face one another either with directly linked computers via local area network [LAN] connections or over the emerging commercial internet), game modding (where the tools for level design were released to the community, allowing them to create maps of their own to play on), and perhaps most significantly

27

from a marketing standpoint the concept of "shareware." Shareware distributed the game on a series of disks or a download that contained only a few levels and required a purchase to play the entire game—in doing so, the footprint of the game was able to achieve what we might call "virality" in more modern times, by means of network effects and low-cost distribution of the software. *DOOM* went on to become one of the most significant titles in the development of early esports, in addition to cementing much of esports gameplay onto PCs.

"The Johns"—Romero and Carmack—emerged from id Software as game design and development luminaries (respectively). Rock star status among highly skilled developers attached to significant games is common in modern game development, but up until this period game developers were often uncredited and not particularly well paid or celebrated. The first Easter Egg (a hidden surprise within a game inserted by the developer) was merely Warren Robinett claiming "created by" credit in the 1980 Atari release *Adventure*, via a hidden room that flashed his name[20] (this also happens to be part of the inspiration for video game pop-culture novel and movie, *Ready Player One*).

While the "Johns" rose to notoriety based upon their immense contributions of their titles, one can credit game development megafirm Electronic Arts for pioneering the "blockbuster" model for game development by celebrating developers and putting a significant sales force and marketing efforts against released titles. In addition to establishing North America as a significant player in video game development (heretofore largely dominated by Japan), Electronic Arts forever changed the way games were designed and sold to a rapidly expanding market of fans.[21] The resulting cycle of development was one that quickly propelled gaming towards a hit-driven industry given the immense production costs of increasingly sophisticated games.

Games were in fact beginning to look increasingly like "blockbuster" affairs not too dissimilar to movies, particularly on PCs. The 1993 release of *Myst* served as perhaps one of the most notable PC game releases in that it was designed to pull in a more mature player by merit of a deep story of intrigue (family betrayals), simple point-and-click puzzle-based game play, and beautiful environments via an emerging PC "trick": namely, CD-ROM drives that allowed for larger data to be played via physical media. The production quality of the visuals, in addition to the increasing sophistication of narratives within some games, are arguably among the major milestones that elevated gaming as semianalogous to other entertainment industries such as film or television, in addition to maturing the themes and conceptual/narrative depth of games. Since the early influences from *D&D* and MUDs, certain genres of games have explored the storytelling qualities of the medium beyond merely completing levels, widening the appeal of games beyond mechanical achievement to completing a story. These shifts would later inspire variable levels of difficulty to allow for wider audiences to experience the full story unhampered by potentially difficult game play. Through the wider entertainment appeal afforded by the story of the game combined with simplified interfaces, *Myst* was one of the first games that an older generation of Baby Boomers (the generation born 1946–1964, which largely did not grow up playing video games) played as their first video game, thereby making an important step towards game design and themes that moved beyond the previously core demographic of male teens from the 1980s and 1990s.[22]

That said, one of the most significant PC-based games of this era had no real narrative to speak of, nor did it require much in the way of technological innovation, though like *Myst* it had the benefit of appealing to virtually everyone. Microsoft Windows 3.0 released in 1990 and included a digital version of *Solitaire* as one of the included applications. One would be hard pressed to find anyone who worked on a personal computer, in a professional or leisure capacity, through the 1990s or aughts who had not played a game or two of *Solitaire* (either as a focused activity, or as a diversion from some other, less fulfilling activity). The relatively humble origins and aesthetics of this game belie a greater significance—*Solitaire* represents a game that had a unique combination of:

- Wide access through a ubiquitous technological device.
- Intuitive controls and rules rooted in cultural understandings of previous game play.
- A noncommittal period for a given play session, allowing for games to be interwoven within daily life (and more likely than not, work life).

Both *Myst* and *Solitaire* have been described as some of the earliest "casual" games (a term and trend we will unpack more directly in the following and final section), and to a degree both have made their unique contributions to "casual" game play, albeit in slightly different ways.

Finally, one cannot consider casual gaming or games on ubiquitous technological devices without mobile phones coming to mind. Though this platform did not reach its stride until the more modern era, the foundations were well established during this period. The first mobile game is credited as the 1994 release of the Hagenuk MT-2000 handset, which included a version of *Tetris*, though much like the history of traditional gaming the breakout hit came years later. In the case of mobile phones, it was *Snake* in 1997, propelled to notoriety in part by the wide availability and popularity of Nokia phones, which included the game. The marketplace for mobile games was only nascent at the time—game development on phones was linked to a specific carrier agreement and device, with only limited means for wider marketplaces for developers to make games.[23] Put another way, game development was largely tied to being included software for a phone rather than being a commodity that could be sold on its own, and therefore it involved tedious developmental practices custom fit for any given phone-specific hardware or software. Innovations in mobile gaming were sporadic and quality variable, aside from oddities such as the Nokia N-gage, a phone designed to straddle the divide of being both a phone and a portable game system, which did neither particularly well. (Sony also announced their own mobile gaming device, the Play Station Portable, in 2003 right around when the N-gage was being brought to market, thereby sweeping a significant chunk of the potential market for an N-gage.)

While the considerable hardware constraints were a non-negligible factor in early mobile game design, the broader philosophy around games that would be acceptable beyond traditional "gamers" is perhaps the most notable differentiation in how mobile game studios operated relative to traditional incumbents. It should come as little surprise that the default strategy for traditional game companies who wanted to enter the mobile space was to purchase mobile studios rather than develop the games with existing resources, given considerable design and technological differences.

The longer legacy of early mobile game development is that it would fundamentally change the orientation of gaming more generally to millions (if not hundreds of millions) of consumers. Within this period seminal games such as *DOOM* were released, which would forever change the trajectory of traditional gaming and esports; yet the "blockbuster" model of game development that emerged at this time placed a challenging burden on the economic viability of game development, and its reliance on hits. Gaming was becoming a serious medium requiring serious talent that expected serious rewards and adulation. Game development was getting very expensive, and the challenges of multiyear development with potentially unknown outcomes yielded a considerable business challenge.

At the same time, more traditional (e.g., *Myst*) and device-packaged (e.g., *Solitaire*, *Snake*) games picked up on the efforts of *Pac-Man* from the earlier arcade era to broaden the applicability and attractiveness of gaming to a larger population, by means of intuitive controls, deeper narratives (*Pac-Man* is credited as one of the first games to have "cutscenes," or little story snippets between levels), and play that could be interwoven into the contours of everyday life by means of flexible play sessions. In short, gaming was primed for the revolution that is playing out even today.

The Casual Revolution (~2006–Now)

The title of this period is borrowed from game scholar Jesper Juul's book *A Casual Revolution*, which described the circumstances of gaming rising to broad acceptability by providing (with some tweaks and liberties we'll be taking for our purposes) a cogent roadmap for understanding the ubiquity of gaming today. Juul points to two driving factors toward this revolution: the increased adoption of mimetic interfaces in games, and downloadable casual games. To the first point, a mimetic interface is one that inputs commands to the system in a way that feels natural to the activity—if you've ever played a *Guitar Hero* "guitar" controller, bashed on a *Rock Band* drum kit, or even picked up a Wii remote, you've used a mimetic interface.

To the second point, we must be cautious—a variety of biases within the gaming industry and the media surrounding it has painted a decided uncharitable and not entirely true picture of what it means to classify a game as "casual." Casual games, and casual players, are often described as folks who simply don't care much about gaming, and don't game much. This is entirely untrue—"casual" game fans can often log as many gameplay hours as a more "traditional" game fan, in addition to having deep, personal (and occasionally, financial) investment in the game. What truly defines a casual game is that neither long game play hours nor investment are required to play. "Casual" should be read not as of passing interest, but as permission towards casual engagement—interactions with a given game or game system in a way that fits the broader constraints of everyday life and competing requirements on our time. By this definition there is a world where even those who play more traditionally designed and oriented games can be described as casual, a nuance that is both true and important towards conceptualizing the current state of gaming and the deceiving overlap between often derided "casual" and "traditional" players.

To do so, we'll add one more angle to Juul's model for the "Casual Revolution" that he addresses throughout the book, though with some more recent updates: the rise of "quality of life" design in gaming. Across all types of games, there is an increased bend towards flexibility—hardware and software designs that allow for a game to be start/stopped in an instant, monetization mechanisms that allow for "shortcuts" towards performances or aesthetic achievements/unlocks, easing how failure is punished in game play, and adjustable levels of difficulty allowing for a broader range of skill levels or cumulative time commitments required to complete a game experience.

Juul describes the "Casual Revolution" as a period when sets of game designers stopped making games simply for themselves, and instead made games for others, thereby ending a long-standing period where essentially a fraction of the potential games audiences was the focus (driven by the "blockbuster" hit or miss nature of historical game development). I would add that game design across the board has become "friendlier," both in terms of the game system and how various hardware innovations have empowered flexibility by relieving the necessity to disproportionately "punish" players throughout the game experience (except when the difficult is entirely the point, such as the infamous "Souls" series of games[24]).

We'll look to roughly 2006–2007 as the launch of this modern era as a confluence of three highly influential occurrences: the release of the Nintendo Wii, the launch of the iPhone (and later the App Store), and the emergence of Zynga as a social gaming powerhouse.

The Nintendo Wii game console was a shot at redemption for Nintendo, who had slipped from being a major powerhouse in the industry coming off the relatively lukewarm reaction to the Nintendo Game Cube, their previous console. The Wii was a return to what had made them so successful in the past—not following the path of the dominating logic within the industry. Coming out of the 1980s crash, Nintendo focused on quality rather than market share, thereby cementing their place as a leader in gaming. With the release of the Wii they were not chasing technological or graphical dominance (à la the Sony PlayStation or Microsoft Xbox), but rather hardware and software that was designed to have broader appeal.

Enter the Wii remote. Then Nintendo CEO Satoru Iwata respected (and perhaps envied) the extent to which daily life revolved around the TV either directly (e.g., viewing) or indirectly (e.g., on in the background).[25] In his mind the Wii, and gaming more generally, could occupy a similar place in the daily lives of all consumers, "gamers" or not. Thus, the Wii "controller" became a motion-controlled "remote," and intuitive motion controls became one of the most notable features of the Wii—allowing for everything from a sword to be swung or bowling ball to be tossed down a bowling alley via controls that just about anyone could pick up pretty easily.

The innovation of the Wii was to implement mimetic controls into gaming technology that had largely been the domain of—and privileged by—knowledge of how to use more traditional game controllers to navigate complex game spaces. Nintendo had long dominated portable console gaming, and just before the release of the

Wii had piloted this same philosophy on the Nintendo DS hand-held console in 2004 (their latest iteration of hand-held consoles, which began with the Gameboy in 1989). Objectively, the DS (short for Dual Screen) was an odd one. The clamshell device opened with two usable screens, the bottom one positioned alongside the more traditional controller inputs serving as a touch screen. This then-novel inclusion allowed for a number of intuitive control inputs, inclusive of "drawing" on the screen with the included stylus.

This era thus kicked off with the "traditional" space of gaming enthusiasts being breached by hardware and software that allowed for flexible inputs that required little or no experience or primary knowledge of gaming via traditional means such as a console controllers. Touch screen controls in particular have become the default mimetic interface for intuitive game control, epitomized by the 2007 release of the Apple iPhone.

Much has and can be said about how revolutionary the iPhone was as a consumer electronics device—we'll stop short of rehashing these adulations in favor of focusing more on the job in front of us: the iPhone allowed for a rich pallet upon which mobile games could be developed and later distributed in a fairly open manner via the Apple App Store (in 2008). Games became as easy to buy as songs from the iTunes store, and in doing so they mostly freed mobile game development from specificity around a given carrier or handset (though the ecosystem has since evolved to the point that most serious mobile developers must accommodate both Apple iPhones via the iOS operating system and phones with Google's Android operating system). Just as importantly, the normalization of touch screens on mobile devices created a ubiquitous control interface for not just the functionality of the phones, but also for the game apps that could be run on them. Distribution and regulation via app marketplaces allowed for wildly popular games such as *Angry Birds* to reach a huge audience drawn in by the fun and family-friend theme

35

of the game, but also served as a neat "trick" the touch screen could perform for the user (dragging back the "slingshot" to propel one of the birds to its pig-army-destroying destiny).

The mobile game landscape that evolved is one that can be defined by a large population of players across titles that are mostly described as "casual." Mobile phones were not, however, the first platform through which games reached massive scale via titles with flexible time commitments and relaxed requirements around player knowledge. For years prior to the launch of the App Store similar games could be accessed through web browsers, though none reached the scale of social-enabled games exemplified by Zynga, by means of smart integrations with then lightning-fast growing social network Facebook. The studio's first title, *Texas Hold 'Em Poker*, was released in 2007, though the massive hit *Farmville* in 2009 is among the first games to rise to the level of mass media. Zynga grew their revenue from $19 million to over $1 billion[26] from 2008 to 2012 via utilization of monetization tactics such as in-game purchases and advertising. However, the relationship with Facebook was short lived—in an ongoing series of platform updates designed to reduce the number of obtrusive "notifications" that these games relied upon to grow the players base (by means of having friends invite other friends to the game for bonuses or currency in games), Facebook systematically shut down the levers that these early "social" games relied upon to reach growth that topped over 80 million users.[27]

Such measures dealt a significant blow to Zynga, which required a number of business model retools that included transferring their core games and business to mobile platforms like iOS and Android, thereby consolidating mobile phones as the de facto platforms for massively scaled play via what are principally "casual" games. These games, and the "casual" players who enjoy them, are an oft derided though thoroughly misunderstood group of game players from the vantage point of more "traditional" game fans on consoles or PCs

36

(a source of much tension among these "gamers," as we'll discuss in subsequent chapters). "Casual" implies a fleeting relationship that is not deeply embedded within the games, though many studies have shown that in terms of hours per week "casual" game fans log many more hours than the traditional ones.[28] Casual games and game fans are also described as having a bias towards "easy" games where victory is assured, but that too is untrue—in a separate study Juul found that mobile game players rated games that were both too hard *and* too easy quite poorly.[29] What distinguishes "casual" games and game fans from traditional ones are how easily the game experience can be interrupted (e.g., mobile games in particular are designed to be played for a few minutes at a time) and flexible penalties for failure (e.g., defeat does not create a large impediment for advancement).[30]

This is not, however, that much different from the trajectory of modern "traditional" games, and hence the problem with classifying games as "casual" when in reality all games (regardless of platform, theme, or type) are adopting more casual sensibilities. This is not to say that casual games have erased the market or development of "traditional" games designed for traditionally defined "gamers" on purpose-built consoles or advanced gaming PCs. Quite the opposite—the complexity, scale, storytelling, and artistry of these games have never been more advanced. These titles have become casual by merit of what are broadly referred to as "Quality of Life" improvements—varying levels of difficulty settings such as "Story Mode" or "Easy Mode" to allow for the full narrative of a game to be enjoyed without prohibitive skill barriers,[31] quick-resume technologies on modern consoles that allow for a game experience to be jumped into within seconds of the previous stopping point, and cloud-based technologies that allow for game experiences—which have historically required dedicated consoles or powerful PCs—to be played on any internet-enabled screen via technologies such as Google Stadia or Microsoft XCloud.[32]

In short, these "quality-of-life" improvements have made games more accessible in both the literal and figurative sense. Cloud technologies allow for games to be accessed outside purpose-built technologies. Flexible difficulties and other game design mechanics that make failure in games less "punishing" partially reflects the freedom that modern memory storage affords for game experiences—many early console games, such as those on the Nintendo Entertainment System, were extremely difficult to make sure that players would often fail, thereby extracting significant play time from a game that was realistically quite small. If you really know what you're doing, you can beat *Super Mario Bros* in about 20 minutes, but most players have never come close to that mark. These changes also partially reflect the reality of designing games even for more time-constrained players outside of the previous focus of the games industry—notably, adults who grew up gaming, but now find this form of entertainment competing with jobs, kids, and other pressures of adult life. The author will point out that he is very much in this bucket, and very much appreciates leveraging "Easy Modes" on occasion.

Mobile "casual" games and the proliferation of mobile gaming is less simply a factor of the wide adoption of smart phones, but rather a shift in game development to unlearn what had been learned for years, where developers would create games that were not designed for those similar to themselves (affluent males), but for any potential player. However, these same traditionally designed games are picking up a number of tactics from the playbook of these casual games, in part because they are simply good design, but in other cases because they are a necessity to retain and attract players beyond teenage boys. In both cases, the convergence of flexible play mechanisms and ways to engage with the game experience mirrored a convergence in monetization strategies around "free-to-play" games driven by historical economic constraints around "traditional" game development.

For most of the history of video games, individual game software has been sold with an upfront cost of ~$50–$60[33] (which therefore often mimics a "razor and blade" economic model[34] in the case of game consoles). This price point has been remarkably sticky throughout the decades, even as costs to produce games have risen dramatically, in part due to the "blockbuster" model of game development noted above and the complex array of talent needed to make games that are graphically beautiful, technologically interesting, and containing deep stories spanning dozens of hours of gameplay. Megahit *Grand Theft Auto V* spent six years in development with costs amounting to $260 million.[35] Some scenarios note that if retail game prices remain stagnant while development costs continue to balloon, any given game title would need to sell in the billions to be profitable as soon as a few decades from now. In this sense, when it was noted above that the traditional model of game development was unsustainable, it is in reference to the ballooning costs on increasingly complex games requiring hundreds of artists and developers across development cycles that cross multiple years, with no guarantee for success, and inelastic pricing options.

Recurrent revenue streams such as subscriptions (either for access to the game or sets of features) and or in-game purchases have borrowed heavily from the free-to-play philosophy to design and monetization, pioneered in part by traditional game developers like Electronic Arts (who were early adopters to "micro transaction" purchase in their sports games) and social developers like Zynga. In the case of Electronic Arts, micro-transactions are a supplemental source of income to offset static sales prices of games. Scaled games such as those on social or mobile platforms often have a huge audience (occasionally numbering in the millions), but the widely accepted heuristic for the percentage of this player base that spends money in the game is ~3–5 percent. Scale is thus a necessity for successful monetization, which offers various game boosters or otherwise for small fees or layers ad units to monetize this audience like legacy forms of media like TV or radio.

In both more "casual" and "traditional" games that leverage free-to-play monetization, what is essentially being sold is the capability to work around or fast-track achievements in the game. In many "casual" games, particularly on mobile, this often comes in the form of in-game boosters to help defeat a particularly difficult level (thereby upsetting norms of meritocracy in game achievement common in the traditional gamer mentality, here again is a theme we'll address more directly later on).[36] In other cases, particularly in more "traditionally" designed games, the dominant philosophy tends to be around purchases of cosmetic items (such as alternative appearances of in-game characters, known as "skins") that often could be otherwise earned through repeated gameplay. By means of not offering an advantage to the core gameplay and instead focusing purchases on non-performance-enhancing content, the presumed sanctity of the competitive game experience is preserved. Recent megahit games such as *League of Legends* and *Fortnite* are both games that maintain appeal among "traditional" game fans while monetizing completely through aesthetic-based free-to-play mechanisms.

The modern era of gaming is thus one where game design stopped ignoring the millions of individuals who had not previously been acquainted with the gaming ecosystem (or had been in youth but had stepped away from the pastime) by means of intuitive controls such as mimetic interfaces, more inclusive themes, and improvements to "quality of life" such that gaming was freed from being an activity where dedicated time needed to be scheduled and instead could be woven into shorter spaces in everyday life. More accessible design coupled with titles across ubiquitous technology has spurred flexible ways for game publishers to transact through equally flexible game experiences. Free-to-play design offset the small percentage of transacting customers with player bases numbering in the millions by means of network effects and vast potential install bases. Everyone is a gamer now, because games are made for everyone.

What's New Is Old: Conclusions

The history of the rise of gaming is a circular one—where we ended up looks a lot like where we started. Games that have intuitive controls, more frequent and low-cost transactions, and design sensibilities that were oriented towards the largest market possible. Along the way, the path was defined by occasionally contrasting economic needs in reference to presumptions around who or what was a "gamer." In the beginning and end of this history, that definition was quite wide, narrowing only in a short but influential period in the 1990s that has heavily shaped the cultural and societal conception of games (particularly among older individuals).

The ubiquity of modern gaming is heir to this long legacy of design and technological convergence towards ways that gaming could be weaved easily into the lives of consumers, in game types that appealed to them, and paid for in measures that make sense for their involvement. In this sense, gaming was put on "Easy Mode" across a number of important axes, and the fans showed up in droves.

Importantly, the ways in which modern gaming reaches and transacts with millions of fans is where the biggest opportunities for outside partnerships can be found. Similarly, understanding the types of game environments that are more or less open to these mechanisms provides guidance as to which types of activations will be most acceptable to the wide and differentiated players across innumerable titles, genres, and platforms. It also brings to light one of the guiding principles of this book—the game industry needs outside partnership for sustainability, and the best partnerships are those based on mutual understanding.

The rise of gaming is in this way a history of the economic, cultural, and technological maturation of the games industry. In this way, it provides a road map for partners to be a part of the rise of gaming in way that is beneficial to all parties involved.

Chapter 3

Why Do We Game?

Gamer Motivations and Psychology

G aming was described as a strategic blind spot in earlier chapters. This spot comes from a multitude of sources, but the biggest and most durable of them are misconceptions around who or what constitutes the gaming audience.

The problem is that many of the existing conceptions around the gaming audience are reductive because they've largely been structured around demographic explanations. This is in part because historically marketers have loved to rely on basic demographic descriptions to account for a great many things. When you strip away the complexities, this is pretty much how ~$70 billion worth of legacy TV advertising was sold for many years. Despite all the "advancements" in understanding consumers in a digital advertising landscape, and all the consumer data captured therein, this trend continues today.

The tale of those demographics is one of the few things that the larger business world can apparently agree on. It's not hard to find a number of oddly similar descriptions of the gaming audience in business-related literature on the topic, even if (somewhat ironically) the reference is a counterpoint for what the gaming audience no longer is: young men in a dark basement, hands stained with Cheetos dust, shirt soaked in pizza grease, pimple-marked adolescent features highlighted from the dim glow of a TV, fully under their command from in-hand controller. Various descriptions of the gaming audience continue to come to this same relative profile not simply because the authors of these statements are lazy, but because the "gamer stereotype" has been impressed in our minds for years.

In reality, your average gaming fan is more likely to be worried about their mortgage than Cheetos dust, and are certainly not uniformly male. The average age of game players across any device is estimated to be 34, and 45 percent female.[1] However, just focusing on the broader demographics of gaming belies three deeper, independent, but related challenges that will be the focus of this chapter and the scaffolding we will use to understand participants in the gaming ecosystem.

First, the media has often incorrectly established the concept of a "gamer" and "gamer identity" through the lens of *moral panics*, a well-documented cycle wherein older generations view any new form of media as corrupting to younger ones. The result is a culture of "outcasts" crafted in a unique period of the 1980s/1990s when gaming was a more closed system to new players, who then felt a great deal of ownership over what was ostensibly one of the most affective forms of media known to man. This in turned reinforced rather intensive amounts of tribalism and "othering" for those who don't conform to the concept of what a gamer is or what proper gaming entails. To address this problem, we'll unravel the nature of moral panics, fandoms, media identities, and participatory cultures.

The propensity to "other" those who most align with the concept of gamer leads to our second challenge. The proliferation of mobile and various other mechanisms that have made games more accessible to larger audiences (often lumped under the "casual gamer" label) led to an identity crisis of sorts among those "gamers." This is the genesis of many of the more problematic behaviors that have been documented within gaming communities (which we will address directly in the next chapter), but also provides the requisite background for thinking critically about how access to gaming and the curtailing of various barriers of entry into the ecosystem has multiplied motivations and tensions within the gaming ecosystem well beyond just "gamers."

The final challenge, having established the requisite cultural and social background, is to outline the fairly well-known psychological impulses that lead to engagement with gaming. We will focus on outlining those that both provide clarity to the "why?" of gaming while being instructive towards the "how?" of integrating with gaming in a positive way (including understanding the not-so-positive parts in Chapter 4).

If it sounds as though we are getting just a bit academic to talk about people who play and watch video games ... well, it's because we have to do so. Believe it or not, the academics really got the jump on the business community in terms of both interest and attention towards gaming, largely in the disciplines of communications, psychology, sociology, medicine, and law.[2] While I'm willing to attribute this to the fact that the type of person who obtains a PhD is very likely to be the same type of person who might be a "gamer" (I'm allowed to cast that stone—I'm in this camp), it's also due to the rather profound ways that gaming has the potential to act upon a number of social and cultural forces. We'll try to skip to the good parts, but we are going to have to check in with the professors a bit.

The pseudo-academic flair we'll introduce here is thus both a recognition of the fact that the business world doesn't have to start out at square one in terms of understanding, but also that the industry is in dire need of moving beyond the superficial. Because gaming occupies an extremely important role in the lives and identities of some, and is on the verge of influencing practically all via potential manifestations of the metaverse, we need to understand it from a cultural perspective. Because gaming has drawn in millions in recent years via a number of different formats and deployments, we need to understand it from a psychological and social basis. Finally, because gaming behaviors will continue to occupy a number of current (e.g., gamification) or forth-coming (e.g., metaverse) mechanisms for communications, a deeper understanding is warranted beyond business communications.

Is a Gamer by Any Other Name Not a Gamer?

You'll be quick to point out that early on in this book I chastised users of the term "gamer," and yet here we are looking at it in black and white. I assure you the point is not to be hypocritical, but to acknowledge that "gamer" is not a completely dead concept, just one that is relevant to only a very small portion of the gaming ecosystem yet is vital for understanding broader motivations therein.

Why did "gamer" even become a label for media consumption, particularly one that seemingly had a much broader reach than labels such as "cinephile" or "audiophile" that might be used to label intense consumers of other forms of media? In the early days of gaming, roughly in the transition from arcades in the 1980s to home consoles in the 1990s, it was a non-mainstream hobby enjoyed by, and marketed to, a fairly narrow band of consumers. As noted in the preceding chapter, what was formerly a medium for all in the form of arcades became quite cloistered and relegated to the plaything of (predominately) children in this era, only to have the audience dra-matically expanded once more in recent years due to a combination of cultural, technological, and generational factors. During this (now seen as an anomalous) period, the term "gamer" became a mecha-nism through which these enthusiasts were "othered" from popular culture at the time. Beneath the radar of popular culture, this group of outcasts became a fandom where the consumption of games became a core part of the personal identity of these participants.

This resulted in a particularly potent form of fandom. The word *fandom* derives from *fanatic*, so in a sense the word already car-ries a negative connotation. The concept of "fan" has been applied to any number of forms of entertainment, including (perhaps obviously) sports. However, fandoms have been described as a "scandalous" category in the assessment of media in popular culture,[3] as it describes those that revel and immerse themselves completely in a form of media rather than establishing objective, aesthetic distance from it. One does not gain mastery or control over the art by maintaining distance, so much as co-opted ownership that comes in the form of "participatory culture," as described by famed media scholar Henry Jenkins.[4]

What makes participatory culture unique is that is makes the line between "producer" and "consumers" of content quite messy— consumers in participatory culture are active and creatively engaged with the medium. This may sound rather underwhelming as one could easily apply this heuristic to social media or any other user-generated content (UGC), but aside from the fact that Jenkins's theory actually predates the consumer internet by about a decade, it's more about co-opting and appropriating forms of media as a vehicle to open up space for marginalized subcultures within dominant ones (more simply—the geeks vs. everyone else).[5] It is the genesis of fan fictions, fan forums, cosplay, walkthroughs, and other mechanisms through which consumers have engaged in a deeper way with a story or form of media. Specific to gaming, the importance of "modding" can be described as a unique from of participatory media where the consumers are at times literally using the tools of the producers to create new forms of art specific to their tastes and needs—fans use game development tools to alter the games themselves. Gaming has been used as perhaps the best or most relevant example within the concept of participatory culture and the blending of lines between producers and consumers.[6]

Participatory culture is thus a useful frame for thinking through fandoms where a high degree of ownership is expressed by the participants and space for "outcasts" is desirable. In some respects, it's the media or cultural studies mirror to the concept of "affective economies"

47

Why Do We Game?

or "affective media," which are more well known in traditional marketing and marketing science.[7] "Affective economies" speaks to customers that are active, emotionally engaged, and socially networked—in some ways creating community within the concept of a brand. While these economies can exist in any form of media that carries an emotional punch (here again, sports and sports fandoms provide a useful example in popular culture), gaming has been argued to be one of the more extreme forms, given the combination of social aspects and portions of the media that are under direct control of the consumer—above and beyond modding, players can make choices in games and potentially feel bad about or good about those choices as they occasionally impact fictional characters.[8]

This is partially why gaming tends to be an extremely potent media format for nostalgia. Nostalgia is strongest when and where meaningful social interactions take place, and games offer both real and fictional degrees of socialization (aided by immense amounts of time and personal investment in shaping the experience, which is often the case with games).[9] This explores the boundaries of social connections when we feel attachment to fictional characters. In a game series like *Mass Effect*, where one of the core game mechanics is making moralistic choices about how to approach a given problem (either a more ruthless "Renegade" response or law-abiding "Paragon"), which often reflects on squad mates whose personalities you come to know and explore over the three tiles and dozens of hours of game play that comprise the main narrative of the series. An analysis by publisher Bioware on a recently released remaster of the series noted that 92 percent of players tended towards the moralistic "Paragon" decisions.[10] While there are potentially a number of reasons for this profound bias, it does demonstrate that game players don't just default to horrible behaviors in games, despite the occasional media framing of gaming (here too, a point we'll return to momentarily), and that being the "nice guy" might be a reflection of care towards these fictional entities. It is often the case that game players speak about experiences in games from a first-person perspective, highlighting their sense of self (and therefore, values and social connections) within the game world as personal and salient.[11]

In short, the term "gamers" represents a category for individuals with deep emotional bonds, and often participatory tendencies, to video games, resulting in high degrees of ownership over the media. Possessions and consumer behaviors inform our personal identities through what psychologist call *self-categorization theory*, which is abundant in consumer affinities that require high degrees of money, time, or effort—here too, something quite unique and particularly attributable to gaming.[12] The resonance of this particular label became sticky during a period in the history of gaming where it was framed as a counter-culture form of media. From there, "gamers" as a label was a way of marginalizing what was construed as frivolous wastes of time (largely by the parents) of 1990s youths, to then be co-opted by that subculture as a way to boundary those that were in or out.

This has in turn led to two challenges for how gaming is discussed in more modern times. First, the narrative around gaming that has been shaped in popular media and overarchingly in the form of various moral panics. Second, the extent to which tribalism around the "gamer" identity has set the stage for a vocal minority of "gamers" to paint perceptions of those that game more generally.

Gaming got a bad reputation for the rather simple reason that it was new, and virtually every new form of media is met with both speculation and fear. While this has been true looking as far back as the printed word, more recently concerned parents have fretted over movies, comic books, or rock music as potentially negative influences over the past 100 years or so. In modern times, social media, gaming, and "screen time" more generally have been the object of moral panics[13]—as youth set out to carve out places for their own

49

Why Do We Game?

culture and experiences; it's met with concerns by parents with too-basic understanding of the existing science on a given social phenomenon, and an unerring feeling of righteousness among an older generation seeking to understand the contours of a younger one.

The predictable cycle of moral panics across generations of communications and media technologies is based in the allure of simplicity—they reduce complex social problems into an easily digestible and addressable scapegoat. The history of gaming is riddled with them, and much can be said about how the very durable stereotypes around the gaming population are due to how the media has narrowly framed the impact of gaming on younger populations (not just to young people, but boys, and in particular boys with a penchant for violence). As those who played games during that anomalous period grew up, and as the population of those who play games expanded via more accessible technology and design, the framing of who plays games has never been more disjointed yet seemingly set in stone—as previously noted, video games are a pastime that largely bends towards adults. We have these moral panics to thank for this incongruity.

When I state (as have others)[14] that the label "gamer" is not useful to describe gaming populations, it's both true and due to this phenomenon. However, this is not to say that those who identify as "gamers" don't exist—it's merely a small part of the overall population of those who play games. Estimates vary but typically hover around 15–20 percent of the population who play video games across any type or device identify as a gamer.[15] The combination of moral panics and the occasionally exclusionary behaviors of those "gamers" have yielded an outsized focus on a small group, thereby skewing overall perceptions.

The exclusionary behaviors of gamers is not something unique to gaming. During the months prior to September 1993, millions of homes across the United States had received a CD-ROM offering software and free trial access to America Online. It was one of the largest and most aggressive pushes of the consumer internet, which had previously been the exclusive domain of large institutions such as universities (if this sounds a bit similar to the beginnings of gaming … it's because it is). As communication channels such as Usenets (a distributed discussion system available on computers at the time) became flooded with new members who were unaware or uninterested in the "netiquette" that had been common among longer-tenured users, this period was dubbed "The Eternal September" or "The September That Never Ended" by those veteran users.[16]

As with moral panics, the patterns of reception and alienation among veteran users in fandoms are not unique to gaming, and in many cases can be traced back for decades.[17] The irony is that many of these fandoms, including those that are cast as "geeky" in popular culture, are often the refuge of cultural outcasts,[18] but it's because these fandoms become safe spaces that new membership feels threatening. Gaming is an acute example given the rapid expansion of gaming populations, particularly via game types and players who were very different from typical "gamers" (i.e., predominately white, middle-class males, playing challenging and/or complex games). This feeling of a threat to a fandom, which many have not just claimed ownership of but have staked their identity within membership, is the root of many toxic behaviors attributed to gaming communities (here too, this is something we'll unpack in the next chapter).

But do we hear from those grumpy Usenet users anymore? Nope, and very likely the less desirable attitudes within the gaming ecosystem will dissipate as a function of time. However, as noted, understanding the larger cultural and social factors around the fandom of "gamers" is an important stepping-stone towards contextualizing gaming behaviors and psychology (good or bad) more broadly. Investment, ownership, and the highly affective nature of the medium means that the psychology of these spaces is somewhat unique, and should be handled with care when introducing new elements (be it ads, technology, messages, or otherwise).

Loops for Loot: Understanding Gaming Motivations

As previously noted, our intention is to focus only on a subset of important psychological phenomena most relevant to the intended audience of this book, although excellent and thorough references from a number of gaming-specialized psychologists exist for further reading (in addition to being referenced throughout this work). We'll do so by outlining the more popular taxonomies around what motivates gaming, followed by some of the more pertinent psychological phenomena attributed to gaming.

The most often cited reference on game play style and attitudes comes from Bartle's[19] taxonomy, which described four types of players in online Multi-User Dungeon games (the progenitor of online role-playing games):

1. **Achievers:** Those who give themselves a goal in the game and set out to accomplish it (be it solve a puzzle, acquire items, complete a level, etc.).

2. **Explorers:** Those who seek to learn the most they can above a given game or virtual world, including the rules that govern it (e.g., in game physics).

3. **Socializers:** Those who use games as a social medium, via role play or otherwise, to interact with other players.

4. **Killers:** This unfortunately named group are those who wish to "impose" themselves on others—they attack other players or otherwise seek to cause distress.

Bartle's taxonomy is widely used because it's not only simple, but neatly categorizes a number of common values and need states within gaming. More recently, Yee[20] built upon Bartle's taxonomy via a large survey of over 3,000 players across a number of online games, which yielded additional precision around the motivations of achievement, socializing, and importantly the concept of immersion:

- **Achievement:** Players seek advancement (gain power, progress, accumulate symbols of wealth or status), competition, and to understand mechanics (analyzing the rules of the game to optimize performance).

- **Social:** Players wish to socialize (helping or chatting with other players), form longer-term relationships, or seek feelings of satisfaction from teamwork via being part of group efforts.

- **Immersion:** Players are driven by discovery (finding and knowing things other players might not), role playing (creating a persona through which they interact with others), customization (the ability to customize a persona to suit personal tastes), and escapism (using the game environment to avoid thinking about real-life problems).

It is probably by no coincidence that the motivations Yee identified closely mimic more general psychological needs and motivations as described by the "self-determination theory" framework.[21] Przybylski and colleagues[22] argue that gaming fulfills three basic psychological needs and motivations:

1. **Competence:** We need to feel skillful and able when we do things.

2. **Autonomy:** We need to feel that we have meaningful choices when deciding how to do something.

3. **Relatedness:** We need to feel connected to others while we do so.

Some important takeaways immediately become apparent between these classifications, with an emphasis on the traits and motivations that seem particularly durable across all three: People playing games are interacting within and through the game. Within the game, it's often related to the joys of mastering game mechanics, becoming immersed in a story and overcoming challenges. Through the game it's a conduit for socializing with others as well as performing identity—game "play" can thus be thought of as both the play interacting within the game world and that which is performative socialization (often with other players, but to a degree also applicable to fictional characters within a game). The drivers above are not exhaustive nor mutually exclusive—what motivates individuals to play games can be highly differentiated from person to person or game to game. This is what, as discussed in the section above, makes games a highly affective medium given differential and deep forms of participation.

Like any type of affective media, this comes with risks—specifically, that bad messaging or tactics can disrupt an otherwise deep and emotional experience, likely resulting in some degree of backlash from the game player. The concept of immersion, known more formally as "spatial presence" by psychologists, is perhaps the most important axis to consider in terms of potential risks within a game (or other highly affective) environments.

Immersion (we'll mostly stick with the less formal parlance, given its popularity in both popular and business-related discourse of gaming) is a psychological state brought on when the boundaries of a media you are experiencing dissolve from reality.[23] Though the concept of "spatial presence" has been studied for decades across a number of different media, one of the principal allures of gaming is the extent to which it can foster immersion via enthralling stories, captivating mechanics, and beautiful graphical displays. Immersion is potentially one of the reasons you're reading this book—because the environments are immersive, game players are highly involved within the game environments both psychologically and physically (e.g., through game controls).

Immersion is disrupted by things that don't fit within the context of the immersed experience. In practice, this is where marketing messaging is most at risk—if it's incongruent to the game environment, it disrupts immersion, and therefore damages the game experience. That said, if the ad or marketing message fits with the environment, it can help with immersion—this is why external messaging placements such as virtual billboards have gained much traction in the world of game advertising, as it's not only acceptable but potentially additive to the game experience.[24] Immersion is further fostered by the concept of "interactivity"—we expect things in a game environment to act as we would expect. "Involvement" with media comes from intensive mental processing of an experience, requiring keen focus and attention.[25] Involvement relies upon the cognitive processes of understanding the game systems, observing problems, and formulating solutions. It's why games are deeply immersive, and gaming more generally is renowned for captivating attention among players.

The shadowy side of immersion, depending on your POV, comes in the form of escapism. Even in the taxonomies above, immersion in a game to avoid the pressures of reality is a potential motivation, but one that is followed closely by concerns around addiction (given a fairly similar need state fulfilled by sometimes abused substances such as drugs or alcohol). That said, escapism can also be understood less as a pathway of avoidance than as something more akin to a philosophical thought experiment—a game can provide virtual worlds to think about and address problems through a variety of vantage points that might not otherwise be possible, against multiple realities and existences.[26] Games have occasionally been purpose-built to this end: *Life Is Strange* is a game where the player essentially explores depression. The act of game play can be immersive to the point of escapist, but the nature of escapism (like many of the negative or positive assessments of gaming on individuals) is nuanced.

Moreover, when games have social elements, it's less about escaping the real world per se so much as contextualizing the real world in new ways. Nick Yee describes the Proteus Paradox as how we often carry meaning, biases, and values from the real world into virtual environments.[27] The "self-perception theory" is a well-known social psychological phenomenon where we tend to contextualize how a third party might view us based upon our appearance and behaviors.[28] Yee and colleagues found that in-game avatars affected player behaviors in and out of game when personal and third party avatars were made more or less attractive, taller or shorter, and so on.[29] Socialization in gaming is, as noted, one of the key need states among those that play games, and takes place in a variety of forms, ranging from direct conversations to teams of players (sometimes formalized within "guilds" or "clans" that confront challenges together). The Proteus Effect explains how we take cues and biases from the real world to influence these socialized behaviors, but the game environment itself can have the same effect.

The process of "deindividuation" is one where we reduce uncertainty in a given social situation by taking cues from the environment, which is particularly potent in situations where our true identity is more anonymous.[30] A positive environment yields more positive behaviors, and negative environments more negative. This process has been used at times by game developers to reduce toxic behaviors in some games—either through "priming" (i.e., pointing someone in a particular cognitive direction) players with positive messages or experimenting in ways to curtail messaging from individuals who were identified as caustic.[31] We'll return to deindividuation and anonymity as they pertain to more negative behaviors; for now we'll merely note that while social interactions are a key motivating function in games, the ways in which they can occur are manifold and subject to influences both within and outside the game environment.

A final aspect of socialization we'll touch on is competition—games are often designed specifically around competing players or teams, often with elaborate systems for comparisons of relative mastery of a given game (e.g., competitive ladders). These are often designed such that players of the same relative skill level can compare mastery with a similar group, thereby allowing for semiobjective assessments of mastery within the right context (e.g., not pitting a middling player against a professional). Mastery of a game is a powerful motivator insofar as it solves for our need to feel competency, particularly when it is tied to the presence of rewards. Games often include "operant conditioning" where performing an action provides a given reward (e.g., click on a treasure chest and you get some gems) and "compulsion loops" where players are compelled to perform the action that leads to the reward given a cue in the game (e.g., presenting a treasure chest, and obtaining the riches therein). These are effective mechanisms for engagement, but it's not a stretch to see how they can lend themselves to abusive behaviors. It's on that note that we'll begin our transition more directly to a discussion of those potentially negative behaviors.

Closing the Loop: Conclusions

Games can elicit a particularly unique form of fandom. The deeply affective nature of the media both draws individuals into the experience, and creates fault lines for divisions. Understanding what motivates participation in this medium allows for more thoughtful consideration of how to influence these environments. This is particularly true here, where influence within the environment is sensitive—there are innumerable risks to breaking immersion in games. Moreover, social and identity dynamics in games can influence the receptivity of the audience, based upon their attachment to the game environment and context through which the players interrelate. Finally, games often rely on well-known psychological triggers to drive engagement and reward mastery. This is in part what makes games so compelling, and therefore can be leveraged to bolster positive integrations in game environments, but this is also where unscrupulous behaviors can potentially ferment.

We've been, on balance, only focusing on the more positive mental processes attached to gaming, only vaguely pointing towards where some of these tendencies lead to darker impulses. We'll address these in the next chapter head on, thereby addressing many of the more common discourses around the psychology of gaming—propensity for violence, addiction, and toxic behaviors. As with understanding the motivations for gaming, the negative behaviors germane to gaming provide a productive path for engaging with these media in a positive way.

Chapter 4

Underworld

Violence, Addiction, Toxicity, Representation, and Brand Safety

For a pastime that's supposed to be fun, gaming has a lot of baggage. So much so that at various points, those in the industry were in favor of removing the words "game" or "gamer" from conversations with those outside the industry, instead relying upon more sterile terms like "interactive entertainment." Public flashpoints like Gamergate, where female game developer Zoe Quinn came under fire based on a factless insinuation from an ex-boyfriend that she had used sex to advance her career, served as a bit of vindication for those who held onto stereotypical conceptions of gamers or the gaming industry. A larger dialogue around representation and biases in gaming ensued, and "gamers" marched out (online, naturally), virtual pitchforks and torches in hand, to attack those in the industry who didn't look or think like them. In seeing a mob of angry young men attacking women, journalists, and nonwhite/nonmale developers, it wasn't a hard cognitive leap to assume that various other qualms directed at gaming fans (that they were violent, addicted to games, nasty to one another or outsiders, etc.) were also true.

Why does it seem like there are so many jerks in gaming? On the one hand, gaming tends to be full of jerks because the world is full of jerks.[1] On the other, much of the toxicity in gaming tends to come from a very small part of the overall gaming population, and developers (along with other enthusiasts) are doing everything they can to

59

stamp it out. Moreover, the science around violence and addiction as it pertains to gaming is, at best, mixed and often misunderstood due to our cultural tendencies to cast new media in an uncharitable light. The result is very skewed perceptions of an entertainment medium that is becoming as common for senior citizens as the raging young men at the heart of Gamergate.

Before delving into all of the above, let's address the elephant in the room. Media scholars and psychologists who address gaming operate in an environment where they are always at risk of being called out as a video game industry shill. Any more balanced (or even positive!) takes on the effect gaming may have on our minds or lifestyles is put under intense scrutiny. I write this book outside of my official obligations to any job or position, and the contents are wholly my own thoughts and opinions, but I am nonetheless (at the time of writing) employed within the gaming industry, and my purpose in writing this book is very much to extol the value of gaming. While I wouldn't go so far as to describe myself as a shill, I would understand a healthy dose of skepticism around my objectivity.

To this end, I express no high degree of authority or expertise on these matters, particularly for the thornier issues related to violence and addiction. Like the previous chapter, I'll be relying heavily on experts and respected scholars such as Pete Etchells, Cecilia Hodent, Jamie Madigan, Christopher A. Paul, Andrew Przylbylski, and T. L. Taylor, among others. For both space and other practical limitations, it will be impossible to give an exhaustive accounting of the scientific debate around these issues, so our focus will be on the high-level overtures with ample starting points provided for those who would like to investigate further.

The intention here is not to flippantly wave away concerns around gaming that are potentially deleterious to entities or individuals entering this space, so much as to highlight what is fact versus hyperbole. Though video gaming has been around for the better part

60

Get in the Game

of half a century, in the history of media more generally it is still quite new. As a result, our tendency to fear the new belies a much more nuanced reality.

Shoot 'Em Up and Beat 'Em Up: Violence and Gaming

In Chapters 2 and 3, we addressed the gaming phenomenon of the 1980s and 1990s, which has largely shaped discussions around gaming. The industry used marketing and game design specifically tailored to their tastes in order to encourage young men in particular to play.[2] Intentionally or not, the result is a long-standing association between young men and gaming that has perpetuated long past the point where it was remotely true for the gaming population. It was right around this same period, specifically the early 1990s, when a series of games being released in part to push the medium beyond merely the pastime of children spurred one of the most influential and important public discussion around gaming.[3] One popular game featuring intense violence (*Mortal Kombat*) and another featuring sexualized scenes (*Night Trap*) sparked congressional hearings around violence and appropriate content in games.[4] Media coverage and political discourse took a sensationalized bent that, similar to the early conception of game fans, has not entirely dissipated some 30 years later.

The immediate result of these hearings is the now-ubiquitous Entertainment Software Ratings Board (ESRB) grading on all games, an industry-regulated system that identifies sensitive themes and age-appropriateness of gaming titles. The longer-term effect was catalyzing the cycle of moral panics around violence and video games, particularly for young men, perhaps best exemplified by the fallout from the Columbine tragedy and the association of this event with first-person shooter videogames.[5] As has been the case with other forms of new media and youth in the past, video games became an easy explanation for otherwise unexplainable behavior. Unfortunately, addressing these issues through the lens of a moral panic often does more harm than good,[6] because it does not do justice to the complex series of causes for a given societal problem. Further, through the lens of moral panics we reduce the conversations around new forms of media to an overly simplistic argument between older generations condemning the behaviors of the younger ones, and younger ones being restricted from mediums of expression because of ill-informed societal or governmental regulation.

Reductive or not, the repetitious conversation around gaming, youth, and violence reinforced what psychologists call familiarity bias, where we think things are true because of dramatization and repetition.[7] Gaming psychologist Andrew Przybylski found that older Americans who didn't really have much interaction with games were almost six times more likely to believe that violent games caused violent behavior.[8] This fallacy becomes particularly problematic when it influences the scientific dialogue around the relationships between violence and gaming. A study surveying over 175 scholars found that the age of the researcher was a significant predictor of attitudes around games (with older being more negative than younger), which only disappear when experience playing games was added to the model.[9] Though the study does not explicitly connect these negative attitudes towards bias in the resulting studies, it becomes clear that understanding of the relationship between violence and games is made difficult not simply through the abstracted lens of moral panics in the larger society, but also the scientific discourse around the topic.

It is probably no surprise that this discourse, even today, remains very unclear (in one direction or the other) in terms of what influence gaming has on violent behaviors. Conclusions on either side of the debate tend to be heavily biased towards baseline discussions on the merit of the methodology of the study, rather than the conclusions of the study itself.[10] Studies are routinely called out for external validity (i.e., do the findings hold up outside of a study environment), due at least in part to the fact that many psychological studies are conducted on undergraduate university students (as a convenience sample). Further, the difficulty in metricizing violence in games is (somewhat humorously) highlighted by a study that attempted to quantify the levels of violence in games with an ESRB "E" rating (suitable for ages six and over).[11] The study found games like *Pac-Man* and *Centipede* to be exceedingly violent, given a rather loose definition of "characters" upon which violence could be inflicted (one of the core mechanics in *Pac-Man* is eating the other characters, after all).

Studies using more established measures such as the General Aggression Model (GAM) have found short-term linkages between playing violent games and priming for violent behaviors (i.e., playing games featuring violent behaviors like punching would then trigger shorter-term biases towards punching others). These studies have concluded that games can put us in the habit of using aggressive actions to deal with a given situation, even if we are not consciously aware of it, and thus identified gaming as a potential risk factor.[12] However, priming tends to be fragile insofar as it is a temporary state, so these results say little for the long- or medium-term effects of games on violent behaviors.

Longitudinal studies (i.e., those looking at these effects over a series of years with the same population under study) have typically shown weak or mixed results. A meta-analysis on longitudinal studies of violence and gaming found only a moderate relationship between violent games and aggression over time, but these effects disappeared when variables relating to prior aggression (or simply being male) were taken into account.[13] A team of scholars in 2015 found that violent behaviors (aggravated assaults, murders, etc.) since 1978 were

63

Underworld

negatively correlated to game sales, inclusive of analysis focusing on the periods following the release of particularly violent games.[14]

Given the rather predictable pattern of moral panics in countries like the United States, it's unlikely that this debate will be over any time soon. Much of gaming scholarship is focused on the effect of violence for this reason, though based on the historical challenges illustrated above it's unlikely that we'll find definitive proof in the near future. In the meantime, what we can safely conclude is that the association is mixed, and popular rhetoric has done much damage to what would otherwise benefit from being a reasonable and balanced line of inquiry. Games featuring violence are incredibly popular and represent some of the best-selling franchises in gaming, but it would be wrong to assume that this is simply due to a darker urge in young men or others towards violent behaviors. These games tend to satisfy many urges attributable to the self-determination theory: they are often challenging, satisfying games to play with occasional elements of sociability.[15]

However, moral panics and parental concerns around gaming have not simply been limited to violence. The potential addictive properties of gaming, particularly in a world where repeated engagements with a game are often a key factor towards monetization, has similarly raised concerns around the relative safety of gaming environments.

Just One More Round: Addiction and Gaming

Watching someone playing a game is not always a particularly thrilling experience—not the action on the screen, but the physical person as they interact with the controller, keyboard, or some other technological interface. To the outside observer, the occasionally unflappable expression on the player's face appears to be that of someone disconnected from reality. In some respects, this is true—in the previous chapter we discussed spatial presence (aka immersion) as the psychological concept where the edges of the game world and the real world disappear, and "involvement" as the processes in our mind engage with media in deep ways. The net result is that video games tend to be consuming media experiences—they engage the mind in a multitude of ways, and the body as it controls aspects of the game.

As a result, the rather deep cognitive and physical engagement required to play a game has all the signals one might expect from someone disconnected from reality in a less savory way—via drugs, alcohol, or otherwise. However, the reality is that games are a medium that are specifically designed to be immersive and interactive—engaging with a game instead of other pursuits doesn't necessarily mean that other aspects of that person's life are deteriorating.[16] The history of other visual media, be it television or movies, has similarly been focused on technologies to increase immersion within that given experience—whether it be larger, wrap-around screens (IMAX) or increasingly complex arrays of speakers to create the illusion of sound coming from any given direction. Games simply tend to be better at it than other forms of media, given the deep involvement required. However, involvement and escapism are close cousins to addiction, which has been the focus of occasional panics around gaming.

Similar to the ongoing debate on violence in gaming, scientific consensus on addiction in gaming has not yet been reached. One of the more impactful positions in this debate was when, in 2018, the World Health Organization included "gaming disorder" in its International Classification of Diseases. This catalyzed a furious debate among the academic community, with counter-points largely revolving around concepts and signs of addiction that might otherwise be a normal or healthy behavior as it pertains to playing a game (for example, the seemingly dissociative behaviors of someone playing a game as outlined above).[17] Much like the scientific debate around violence, the appropriate measures and challenges related to collecting causal data on the phenomenon of addiction have yielded a conversation more around methodologies and metrics than about what, if any, problems exist (including what are the most effective routes to treat the problem), and how common such problems truly are. Estimates of the true prevalence rate vary widely (from a few tenths of a percent to nearly half the potential gaming population).

The high degree of abstraction and incertitude in the scientific community on this topic, coupled with moral panics, raises barriers that make addressing more fundamental issues challenging—particularly when government action is involved. Such measures of control can, at times, be more harmful and impractical than helpful. As recently as 2021, China announced a crackdown on gaming for Chinese youth, where anyone under 18 is allowed to play games for just 3 hours a week.[18] Given the skill that youth in China have developed to circumvent various government restrictions, it's unclear how effective these measures will be, but these restrictions demonstrate a case where a sovereign government finds itself in an impossible tug-of-war by wanting to invest in the internet or other technological literacy while maintaining political stability by promoting conservative values. More simply, they are attempting the near-impossible and thereby inflicting near-impossible-to-enforce regulations on their youths.

Though these measures were ostensibly put into place to address a widespread problem with addition, addiction as manifested through mediums like games is often rooted in deeper disorders—taking away the technological layer doesn't solve the underlying condition (in some cases it may make it worse). Such interventions also strip away the benefits of gaming. In reaction to the COVID-19 pandemic, the World Health Organization (the same one that defined "gaming disorder" a few years earlier) recommended that individuals play video games together as a way to maintain social ties when physical proximity was impossible,[19] along with a media campaign encouraging people to #PlayApartTogether. Much like the scientific debate around gaming, regulation via governments and institutional bodies continues to be mixed.

This is not to say, however, that addictive tendencies within gaming do not represent real risks that can inflict material harm. As previously discussed, compulsion loops in games are mechanisms that through operant conditioning (when we are trained to do something, because that thing will yield a reward) we are compelled to repeat series of actions (go through a game dungeon, find treasure chest, etc.) for a reward. Moreover, when these rewards are randomized and unknown, we're cognitively hardwired to be all the more interested in the potential outcome. These loops are often the core mechanism to many popular games. However, these mechanisms are not entirely different from the basic psychology of a slot machine, which is the basis for much of the concern around addition and video games when the mechanics in video games emulate those of gambling. Similar mechanisms are the basis of monetization tactics in many games—"gacha" games (named after the Japanese toy vending machine) provide randomized and unknown prizes for spending in game currency. Micro-transactions in games often include "loot boxes" that operate under a similar premise—a player spends money to get an optional and unknown bonus to the game experience. There is ample room for potential concern when game designers deliberately exploit these psychological tendencies for financial gain.

Psychologist and game UX expert Celia Hodent warns of "dark patterns" in game UX design.[20] A dark pattern is when design includes deceiving functionality to maximize profit at the expense of a user. Such patterns can be found in games relying on exploitation of known psychology to maximize revenue. However, even reputable game studios that rely on micro-transactions have the potential

67

to encourage spending behaviors that come perilously close to such exploitation. To be clear, there is nothing inherently wrong with "gacha," "loot boxes," or other similar mechanisms—how they are valued and positioned to the player can mean all the difference between an appropriate transaction vs. one that benefits from compulsion. It should also be recognized that many players who spend via these mechanisms, even occasionally in large amounts (often referred to as "whales"), do so fully cognizant of the costs and largely as an expression to support a developer they value.[21]

Addiction and violence as they relate to gaming are thus two very important topics where needed conversations have been stunted by heavy-handed intervention from the press or government institutions, and scientific consensus is hampered by a number of issues common to the conduct of rigorous science. The resulting mix leads to an understandable amount of concern from outside entities. As noted, outside of specifically malicious intent baked into a game, the linkages between playing games and violent tendencies or addiction are vague, and will remain an ongoing and long-standing debate.

These debates can occasionally be amplified by the fact that, well, portions of the gaming community can be really hard to sympathize with. Specifically, gaming has become somewhat notorious for housing communities that are particularly toxic and exclusionary, leading to persistent issues of representation in gaming (and by proximity, esports).

Git Gud: Toxicity and Representation in Gaming

The "chat" in certain games or gaming communities (the voice or text discussion overlaid on the game play) has occasionally become a thing of legend, or more accurately, notoriety. Exchanges in certain corners of the gaming community, ranging from specific games to generalized platforms like Twitch, are filled with the occasional good-hearted ribbing ("git gud" is an invitation for players to "get good," or improve upon poor play) one might expect from competitive chatter, but often teeters into the realm of excessive obscenities and slurs directed at specific groups—notably women and minorities. The mere presence of a female voice on a gaming chat-enabled service like Xbox Live evokes upwards of three times as much verbal abuse as a male voice.[22]

It's probably unsurprising that as a result, certain aspects of gaming have a representation problem. Moreover, this is in some respects relished by small, virulent parts of the gaming community that hold specific beliefs around what does or does not constitute a game, what is or is not a proper way to play a game, and therefore who is or is not a "gamer." The participatory culture around the fandom of gaming, as discussed in the preceding chapters, entails a high degree of ownership over the medium by portions of the fandom. When this ownership is mixed with what psychologist Christopher A. Paul calls "toxic meritocracy" built into how games are designed and brought to market, it is a particularly noxious mix.[23]

Paul argues that gaming is a place where the ideology of meritocracy runs rampant, seemingly unaware that accumulated and transferable skills from game to game have been enabled by game designers that had for many years designed games with an ethos of making them "for gamers" as the only viable demographic for game play. The resultant culture is one where skill within the game is privileged above all else, without awareness for why others might not have the same familiarity with game systems to be similarly "skillful." The period in the 1980s–1990s where gaming was specifically focused on young men essentially cemented that same group, who were affluent and privileged enough to play games in their free time, as the default "gamer" group.[24]

Skillful game play was encouraged by design—early arcade and console games from this period were designed to kill you quickly,

69

Underworld

either as a means towards monetization (defeating the player would often yield another quarter),[25] or through memory limitations (games could be small in size so long as it was hard to make much progress). Merit in games was thus assessed by those that had the economic ability and cultural permission or encouragement to play games. Those same players would thus go on to be game designers, creating what was essentially an echo chamber of this set of "gamers" making games in the vision and of the design that most conformed to these sensibilities, including characters and themes that would be interesting and relatable to this same set of young, affluent, and predominately white men.[26]

As gaming rose in prominence, and new populations had access and monetization methods that conformed better with their needs and expectations in gaming (as discussed in the earlier chapter on the rise of gaming), this formerly insulated community came under threat. In particular, many mechanisms in free-to-play games were reviled by legacy gaming fans as they represented a departure from supposedly merit-based skill norms—thus, free-to-play mechanisms that provided a material advantage (for example, things like boosters) were derided as not real games, nor those that played them real "gamers." Ironically, counter to this fetishization of masculinized skill among legacy gamers, the most acceptable mechanism for free-to-play from this group comes in the form of purchasing skins and other cosmetics or clothes for their virtual avatars in games like *League of Legends*.

The vitriol from this group fostered a complicated relationship with women in particular, who were more likely to find the themes and mechanisms of free-to-play games (predominately on mobile phones) to their liking, including lighter and more positively oriented aesthetics and settings more often found in casually oriented games. However, women resisted being associated with anything "casual" because of the negative implications in the more "traditional" gaming culture.[27] But even when they enter these more traditionally skill-based game spaces, the reaction is hardly welcoming. As noted above, female voices in these game environments were lighting rods for harassment, a phenomenon that was particularly amplified when the harasser is losing.[28] Here too, the reaction is one of threat—in this case, around a concept technology-oriented sociologist T. L. Taylor associates with competitive gaming known as "geek masculinity."

Geek masculinity is essentially a counter to traditional sports or athletic cultures as a requirement for masculinity, inclusive of the physical activity of the sport itself. It is facilitated by interest in competition and relationships in alternative formats like video games. In this light, dominance is asserted by demonstration of knowledge and competency or skill within these environments. As women increasingly enter these spaces, they are fundamentally upending these systems of exclusion by threatening the status markers that men were relying upon to secure their masculinity.[29] In this way, a subculture that has occasionally been the refuge for social outcasts adopts behaviors that are as exclusionary as the ones they may have faced in popular culture—all for the purposes of preserving identity around a fandom through which they have high emotional and personal attachment.

When developers and journalists contribute to the othering of these groups and modes of play, particularly in the assessment of how skill is a superior mechanism for assessing games, the attitudes of these players are reified by the larger social and cultural constructs within the gaming ecosystem.[30] The previously discussed example of Gamergate[31] once again serves as a poignant example, where female developers and journalists were largely under siege by the toxic elements of the gaming community for raising issues of inclusivity and making spaces for women in gaming. The reactions ranged from verbal abuse to physical threats against these women, thrusting the problem of representation and toxicity within gaming into the limelight, a problem that reverberates even today.

In summary, the increased presence of those not conforming to the idealized "gamer" challenged the very foundational identity of those who consider themselves "gamers," leading to a high degree of toxicity and to considerable barriers for those not conforming to this identity (women, minorities) to integrate in a meaningful way. Toxic behaviors proliferate in gaming platforms due to the often deindividualized and anonymous ways in which communications can develop on these platforms—without fear of reprisal, the ugliest beliefs someone might hold are free to come to fruition.

However, it is not unreasonable to say that things are improving, and all hope is not lost despite the downsides of gaming and the undesirable elements of the game community. Much of this due to the efforts of both game publishers and gaming enthusiasts.

Clearing the Dungeon: Conclusions

Gaming has often been an area where marketers or decision makers were given great pause on the basis of brand safety, largely due to the negative connotations around violence, addiction, toxicity, and the potential impact of these factors on associated brands or entities. Though daunting, the wildest concerns around these aspects are more likely attributable to erroneous characterizations in the media. The science around violence and addiction is, as noted, incredibly mixed—definitive linkages and conclusions are few and far between due to intense methodological challenges. The net result is that we cannot be completely assured that gaming has no negative effects in these respects, but one should similarly not dismiss possibilities within the ecosystem based upon hyperbolic claims that have little factual basis.

A recurrent theme in this book is that the design intention of the publisher matters, and like many considerations in gaming, the best solution is to vet and partner with reputable publishers who prioritize the player experience. This not only provides some shielding from "dark patterns" in game design that can encourage harmful spending on the behalf of players, but can also provide assurances as to where the publisher is actively working against issues such as toxicity. Developers of games that have more toxic communities have implemented a series of measures, ranging from chat censoring to player-rating systems, to counter expressions of toxicity. Riot Games, developer of *League of Legends*, has gone so far as to create a cross-disciplinary "Team Player Behavior," complete with game psychologist, to refine game experiences and systems to minimize toxic behavior.[32] The agency of the larger gaming community is important—as aside from a generalized desire to be rid of the worst elements of the community (who, let's face it, are generally not that fun to play with), it keeps the developers in check. Pushback on predatory monetization practices that are often aligned with randomized elements that can foment addictive behaviors is often quick to spark a furious response.[33]

Basically, nearly every side of the gaming ecosystem is working to keep the worst tendencies of gaming in check. That said, considerable work remains to be done—many of the factors contributing to toxicity in the game environments have similarly shut down opportunities for women and minorities to engage with esports in a meaningful way, and no system is perfect at eliminating toxic behaviors. And yet, moving towards larger, more open ecosystems means better player experiences, more revenue for game developers, and (presumably) more and better games. Those wishing to align with gaming should be cognizant of these risks, but assured that that the expansion of the gaming ecosystem is predicated on all actors being incentivized to make it better.

Chapter 5

Getting in the Game (without Changing It)

Gaming Integration Opportunities for Businesses

O f the many goals we have set forth, the most basic one is to both increase understanding and learn about opportunities within gaming and esports. With nearly three chapters on understanding, leading to one on integration, it may feel as if the balance has been someone lopsided. This is indeed the case, and deliberately so.

The lead-up was not only meant as a means to increase your understanding around gaming as an ecosystem more generally (though this is important!), but also provide the requisite foundation to address opportunities in gaming in a way that is realistic, informed, and with expectations managed. If the ask was to emblazon the hottest AAA game with a brand logo, I'm sorry to note that you will be disappointed. However, the intensive degree of focus that gaming evokes from players means that something a bit more nuanced can go a long way (and there is still ample room to go splashier; it's just going to take more work than you might expect).

This is largely due to the fact that, as demonstrated in the chapters leading up to this point, gaming is a form of media the evokes a different form of attention and participation from its audience, has typically been at the crest of technological innovation and used as a mechanism to understand these technologies, and has developed an increasingly sophisticated and diversified array of strategies to draw in revenue based upon the unique economic challenges of game development. Whereas the coin drops of early gaming gave way to larger upfront purchase in the form of buy-to-play cartridges, the relative inelasticity in the price point consumers were willing to pay to buy into any given game experience has yielded strategies ranging from subscriptions to free-to-play games supported by advertising or coin-drop-sized purchases.

In some respects, the opportunities for outside integrations into gaming have become particularly rich as a direct result of the multiple ways in which the broader gaming industry now transacts with its customers. The traditional model of revenue generation within gaming has become unsustainable,[1] and partnerships are a mechanism through which development costs can be subsidized. However, like so many other aspects of gaming that have a longer history than many might suspect, advertising or other marketing partnerships are not a new phenomenon.

Since at least 1978 ads have been featured in games (in the title *Adventureland* (which contained an ad for the developer's next game, sensibly enough), and the 1980s and 1990s were peppered with both static in-game advertising and the occasional game designed to principally be an advertisement for a brand (an advergame, which we will discuss in more detail later). The fact that many of these previous executions are not well known has less to do with industry-wide blind spot around gaming, than the fact that these early examples were not particularly successful.

In the pre-internet era of gaming, advertisements or brand placements had to be permanently hard-coded into the game. This not only created a tremendous creative conflict for game developers (advertisements may not fit well within the game environment) but was quite out of step with how brand partnerships are typically formulated, given that most advertising buys are structured around temporally defined campaigns, meaning permanent placements were unattractive. In the most extreme examples, brands circumvented the developer issue entirely by making games on their own, although at considerable costs and potentially unknown returns.

The net result is that for many years, opportunities in gaming did not provide much flexibility for partners, were profoundly limited in scope, and/or required tremendous amounts of monetary or time investments. Outside interest in integrating with games was thus relatively fleeting early on, a feeling that was quite mutually shared with game developers and platforms, who either could not or were not inclined to work around the conflicts that outside entities represented when present in their games, except for the very few contexts where an outside entity would make sense in the potential game worlds.

In subsequent years beyond these early forays, the scale and scope of the gaming industry have become too large for potential partners to ignore while the diversified business models adopted by the gaming industry have allowed for more surface area for more natural, flexible, and beneficial integration points for partners. In other words, integrations into gaming have become more desirable because the value and potential return for all parties have aligned in a mutually beneficial manner (including the game players in the best-in-class examples, which we'll discuss later herein).

In summary, recent attention around the potential for brands and businesses to integrate with gaming has been renewed, driven in part by:

- Wider adoption of free-to-play models in gaming, which both raised the size of audiences to the scale of media and allowed for more flexible economics that outside entities could tap into.
- The relatively small number of individuals who spend money in free-to-play games, leaving an open canvas for more passive

two-sided business models (i.e., advertising-supported) similar to what TV or print has relied on for years.

- Rising popularity of game IP to be on par with more traditional entertainment franchises, making broader partnerships outside of the game environments more attractive to outside entities.

- Advancements in technologies allowing for more realistic game worlds, providing better context for outside entities, which may (ideally) increase the quality/realism of the game environment,[2] and connective technologies allowing for diversification in messaging placements.

However, as much as the opportunity space has expanded, the potential concerns and considerations from what differentiates a successful vs. an unsuccessful integration into the gaming ecosystem have become no less challenging. If anything, one might argue that the depth of the game experiences and associated fandom has created more rather than less considerations that interested partners must bear in mind.

As such, the approach here will not overly focus on tactics so much as an outline of broader strategic considerations for integrations in reference to important takeaways from preceding chapters related to game psychology (including both motivations and toxic tendencies), brand safety, and the economic history of gaming. This allows for a generalized approach that can be leveraged against any given tactical execution (though useful starting points will be highlighted throughout), culminating in a tool kit of strategic vantage points, which lends itself equally well from ad buys in games to contextualizing future opportunities in prospective platforms or environments such as the metaverse.

Our discussion will be directed across three broad categories that remain relatively similar to the opportunities presented in gaming some 40 years ago, roughly arranged from the easiest to the least easy to execute and lowest to highest organizational lift on behalf of both the gaming partner and game developer:

1. **Game Advertising:** Placing ads in games has come a long way in recent years, via the advent of dynamic placements coupled with flexible means of purchasing spots via programmatic ad buying. Integrating into gaming can be as simple as buying an ad not entirely unlike how one might do so for any other digital property.

2. **IP Partnerships and Sponsorships:** Leveraging IP that resonates with consumers has been a fundamental strategy within the broader entertainment industry for years, and gaming is no different. As the power and ubiquity of some game IP surpasses that of Hollywood, gaming partnerships and sponsorships have the potential to resonate with an increasingly wide array of fans, including unique ways to funnel player value back into the game environment.

3. **Gamevertising/Advergaming:** At first glance, there would appear to be no better way to get into gaming in a serious way than, well, making a game. While a number of brands have managed to make this leap, an understanding of the fundamental challenges around game development allows for a more informed basis to make this leap. For the sake of comparability, we'll also include "playable" ads in this category (as strategically/logistically, these are more like an advergame than a transactional ad buy using videos or static images).

Our goal is to not be comprehensive so much as to craft an informed, strategic foundation that encompasses the most popular and viable mechanisms to integrate into gaming (as noted, esports are absent as a topic here, but we'll address the subject more fully in the next section). Though the general form that integrations may take has not changed dramatically over the years, this is not for a deficit of creativity—what we'll find is that the depth and diversity of potential activations within this category have become profoundly multifaceted, yielding a comfortable and valuable fit for nearly any brand, industry, or consumer-type to be reached.

Virtual Billboards in Virtual Worlds: Advertising

Gaming has never been a staple in the diet of media buyers. This is in part due to the cumbersome ways in which advertising interacted with gaming in the past—rigid, often ill fitted, and lacking the transparency of other more flexible forms of media. While not necessarily all that different from legacy media of the same age (TV, outdoor billboards, etc.), the emergent nature of the media and presumed narrowness of the demographic (recall that gaming was largely marketed towards—and designed for—young men in the early days) meant that the all-important weighting of ROI seemingly never quite checked out.[3]

Fast-forward to the digital age, and much has been done to change the perception of ad buyers around media more generally—expectations around real-time updates on performance and deployment of campaigns have become the norm, with digital-native platforms such as social media rising to the occasion, whereas more legacy forms of media such as television have largely had to rely on industry inertia to drive growth. As an inherently digital media, gaming has not been out of step with this shift—many gaming platforms and networks deploy best-in-class reporting, ad tracking, measurement, and methods of buying. And yet, the one thing that seemingly has not changed is media buyers' appraisal of the demographic, which remains frozen in time to those early days of advertising opportunities within gaming (the average age of game players largely aligns more to key shopping demographics than to teenagers).

As discussed in the opening chapters, it is precisely this miscalibration on behalf of media buyers that was the inspiration for this book. Not only is the audience in gaming sufficiently large to be appealing for advertising buys, but the unique engagement that players have with gaming over other options in digital media has the potential to position gaming as one of the most potent forms of digital media in the current ecosystem.

A bold claim to be sure, but one which has been largely backed by data, despite the perils of putting too much stake in industry-facing ads research. Almost all studies have an agenda and few with a defensible methodology (once again, I get to cast this stone, as I worked in ad research for many years), so we'll focus on overtures rather than specific numbers: most studies have found that game players would rather give up other forms of media than their games, prefer ads in contexts such as mobile games over other places on the internet, and find that the better-fit placements in games (such as rewarded video, which we will address momentarily) are less distracting/annoying than other ads, in addition to being generally preferred by consumers and marketers relative to other ad placements.[4] Though cross-channel comparability tends to be a tricky topic, there is a growing set of examples where advertising in game environments outperformed contexts such as social media that have enjoyed more significant adoption in the marketing world.[5] Without much in the way of opportunity for user-generated content (more on that when we discuss opportunities in streaming/esports in Chapter 9), gaming tends to lean toward being quite brand safe (i.e., unlikely to place an ad within objectionable content, likely to place it within the right titles) and the incentivized structure of the more successful placements leads to high viewability and completion of video ads.[6]

Getting in the Game (without Changing It)

Naturally, there are some important caveats to these upsides—the biggest one perhaps being that not all games and not all ad formats are going to work. Despite some recent innovations such as endeavors to serve ads against console-based games,[7] most of the discourse on game advertising focuses solely on the opportunity within mobile games. The reason for this focus is twofold. First, mobile games command the largest audience, by far. For all the talk in the advertising industry on needing to focus on effectiveness, it very much remains a scale-oriented game. Second, mobile games have almost universally had to rely on free-to-play mechanisms in order to catalyze user growth. As a result, the design of the game and expectations of the users are significantly more aligned towards accepting exogenous messaging than, say, a game on PC or console.

This is due in part to a tug of war of sorts between the expectations of game consumers versus the needs and ways in which game developers extract revenue from their product, where the most contested areas have been micro-transactions (smaller, occasionally randomized optional content for the game), downloadable content (DLCs, or more substantial parts of the game made available and separate from the core game), and the presence of advertising or other business integrations. The presence of these occasionally contested components to the game tends to be offset by incentives and by how the consumer has been oriented towards transacting with the game experience. Higher incentives in games lend themselves to more willingness to accept non-game elements (such as an ad)—put simply, game players may be willing (or even eager) to view marketing messaging assuming there is tangible benefit payout for them.

The bar for this value will tend to be quite a bit lower in a free-to-play environment relative to a game experience where the player had to pay for the game upfront (which is most common in PC or console games). That is not to say that it's impossible to bridge this divide, but the incentive given to the player would almost certainly need to be profoundly valuable, and games outside of the broader free-to-play orientation often don't have complex (or any) game economies to support incentives that could be flexible enough for value provided to the player relative to the cost to the partner.

Put more simply, free-to-play games will require less value to be demonstrated to the player and have a multitude of ways to do so; games with upfront costs almost certainly will not, and the value to the player will have to scale accordingly. This is partially due to player disposition—if they've already had to pay money into the game, the idea of paying more directly (e.g., microtransactions) or indirectly (e.g., ads) will tend to be unappealing. This creates differential value needs from the onset, and this value comes with tangible costs—something that is valuable to the player is also something that could potentially be sold by the developer (up to and including the upfront cost of the game). For the transaction to be worthwhile for the developer, the cost to the partner may be well out of range for competitive costs via other advertising channels. Free-to-play games often have economies that are flexible enough, and player expectations aligned to where the bar for needed value is sufficiently in step with the potential costs for partners.

As an illustrative (albeit, hyperbolic) example, it's a generally safe bet that a gaming fan would be willing to watch just about any ad you give them (for almost any length of time) if you were to subsidize a $60–70 game title for them, but chances are that would not yield effective economics for you, the partner. This is the extreme end. As we move to the less extreme end, we may find costs only amount to a few pennies per view of an ad, assuming the following:

- That the players' expectations are aligned with this experience (as is the case with free-to-play)
- That there is sufficient inventory/audience for the tonnage of views required for such strategies to be worthwhile to the developer (as is the case with mobile)

- That the game environment has multiple vectors to transact value via a more sophisticated game economy

As blockchain and cryptocurrencies become more commonplace in gaming, the term "game economies" will likely take on a number of different meetings, but for now it refers to the various currencies and rewards that a player can earn or be awarded within a game environment, usually manifesting in three broad forms:

1. **Soft Currencies:** Easy-to-acquire forms of currency in the game, usually earned readily as part of the core game play experience, which are typically exchanged for minor or temporary rewards or game boosts.

2. **Hard Currencies:** Currencies that can buy substantial game rewards or advantages, usually doled out in much smaller amounts than soft currencies to encourage acquisition by players via an in-app purchase (IAP).

3. **Durables:** Permanent rewards that can be earned by a player, often in the form of "skins" or other "cosmetic" items that players can accrue and utilize within a game indefinitely.

What specific form that these currencies appear as varies from game to game (soft/hard currencies might be coins/gems in one game, normal/power crystals in another, etc.), but the underlying logic and relative valuation between them are reasonably common across game economies. Mobile games tend to have economies that support both soft and hard currencies (and occasionally more), allowing for finer control in terms of how rewards can be given to the player (and therefore, multiple ways in which outside entities can become involved in distributing awards to players), whereas even free-to-play games common to consoles or PCs will tend to rely on durables or a singular, "hard" form of currency. This does not mean that integrations are impossible, but rather that the value of the rewards will be both high and inflexible relative to mobile titles, making the costs almost certainly too prohibitive for advertisers at this time (and not giving developers much of a reason to develop access for advertisers). Conversely, given that soft currencies carry less value within the game economy, distributing amounts for (say) every ad view, or a time-limited booster, tends to be a lightweight way for games to incentivize ad views without cannibalizing revenue from potential IAP sales or otherwise disrupting the game economy (bad for the developer) or mechanics (bad for the player, insofar that a huge influx in high-value hard currencies could effectively trivialize a game).

The focus on rewards, acceptability of incentives, and relative bars set for acceptable incentives is deliberate. The psychology of gaming is unique in that it demands disproportionate attention—this is advantageous for outside entities that endeavor to have a game player pay attention to a given message, but comes with the price of requiring benefits paid to the player for this diversion from the otherwise all-attention-encompassing game environment. As such, we'll find that incentives of some type or another tend to form the foundation of any successful outside integration within gaming, but this remains particularly true for an integration which cannot seamlessly be folded into the game environment, such as adverts.

This is not to say that advertising without incentives does not exist—a number of "interstitial" or "adjacent" placements that occur around the game environment are common:[8]

- **Rewarded Video:** Ads that provide an incentive upon completion of a completed video of an advertisement.
- **Interstitial Ads:** Ads that occur between levels or other in-game activities, often without an incentive.

- **Display Banners:** Static ads that appear as a constant through-out the game experience, typically anchored to the bottom or top of the game environment.

- **Offer Walls:** A series of in-game incentives offered to the player for other activities ranging from viewing an ad to sign-ing up for a service.

Though placements will come in a variety of flavors including various options as to whether the player can opt in to an ad or not, pending the game publisher or network, these represent the most common archetypes. The relative scale achievable by the placement, and cost will tend to vary accordingly, with more player-forward options such as opt-in rewarded ads being costlier than simple ban-ners, which share many of the same problems of traditional ban-ners from the early days of internet advertising (people ignore them, more or less).

Both asking for permission to interrupt the game experience (i.e., opt in) and rewarding the player for the diversion of attention tends to be the best-in-class mechanism that currently exists for a player-friendly ad experience. Ones that interrupt or block the game expe-riences (such as some applications of interstitial ads or offer walls) or in some way break the psychological process models of spatial presence/immersion will evoke a negative reaction from the game player and are therefore ill advised.[9]

Incentives are therefore a key component of the integration strategy with games from a direct advertising perspective, and figure heavily into broader sponsorship or partnership opportunities out-lined below. Conversely, advertisements that fit with a given game environment can in some respects aid the process model that a player uses to be immersed in a game, and therefore carries ben-efits to the game experience beyond the need for incentives. These "intrinsic" ad placements, where advertisements are weaved directly into the game experience, offer an alternative avenue for best-in-class integrations.

Some of the earliest advertisements within game environments in EA's FIFA International Soccer in 1993 featured branding from Adidas on the sidelines—though these placements conformed to the logic of the game experience, they lacked the aforementioned flexibility privileged in modern media buying. Internet connectivity in games has allowed for similar virtual billboardesque in-game or in-play advertisements to be dropped into games in a way that seems natural to game play environment (e.g., literal billboards in a racing game), which can be dynamically swapped based upon ad servers connected to any given advertising supply source. However, because these advertisements may only be on screen for a limited amount of time (perhaps for about as long as it takes for a race car to whip around a corner) they'll lack the full-screen and multisecond impact of an incentivized video advertisement. At the time of writing, I'm not aware of any research that has looked at the comparative advantages of engagement with a game environment against a relatively quick/intrinsic view of an ad vs. the more direct, incentivized route. As advertising engagements with gaming become more sophisticated, I anticipate that the fidelity of insights around the most effective placement and strategies will become as rich and common as those against search, social, or other digital channels.

In the meantime, the net result is that there is no perfect strategy, but rather a number of viable routes pending the goal of the advertiser. Game advertising placements can be bought directly with publishers (particularly those with a large mobile gaming footprint), through various ad-tech companies, which are increasingly specializing in placing in-play advertisements, or even large programmatic ad exchanges that incorporate inventory from mobile games. Similarly, the wide breadth of genres covered in mobile games allows for flexibility in terms of the desired audience to be reached. Puzzle games (particularly of the match-3 variety, where various jewels or other baubles of the same color must be aligned by the player) tend to be favored by older women, younger men tend to prefer mobile shooter games, whereas action or adventure games tend to fall somewhere between. Ultimately, working with a given game publisher or game advertising network to understand the potential audiences that can be reached will be paramount, though understanding the advantages and disadvantages of placements in a given game environment will provide an important strategic advantage for selecting the right means of integration.

This Game Brought to You by ... : IP Partnerships and Sponsorship

The most considerable advantage (and disadvantage) of in-game advertising is that it occurs within or around the game environment. Understanding how the psychology of game play interacts with this experience will have tremendous bearing on the receptivity of the advertisement, and the extent to which a given game developer is willing to onboard these experiences relative to preserving the creative integrity of the game. The most common solve for the potential intrusion of an exogenous message is to provide value to the player as an incentive in the game environment, or weave the message into the game environment in a manner that does not breach immersions.

Broader IP partnerships and in-game sponsorships are a common path to integration that follows a similar logic, either by means of taking the advertising outside of the game environment (in the case of IP partnerships) though potentially still tied to an incentive, or working with a developer to create an experience that is more directly tied to the game in a naturalistic way. In both cases, some of the burden of fitting within the game environment is offset either by means of removing the game environment from the equation or working more directly with the game developer to do so in a way that is deeply tied to the game experience. However, neither are as turn-key as game ads, often requiring direct partnership agreements with the gaming partner and development resources (whereas in many cases in-game ads can be purchased through advertising networks or other ad-technology entities that aren't even directly involved in game development and/or offer a number of other choices for advertising inventory). Once again, either option presents opportunities and tradeoffs depending upon the needs and expectations of the outside partner.

IP partnerships or corporate alliances, for our purposes, point to utilization of a given game or game publisher marks or characters/environment/etc. for promotional purposes outside of the game environment. This includes the integration of these assets on product packaging, in cross-promotional materials, or otherwise. As far as business integration tactics go, this one is perhaps the most standard across any number of different industries or media types; however, utilization of game IP has a number of distinct advantages relative to (say) a similar execution using IP from an upcoming movie or other comparable from the broader entertainment industry.

First, game IPs have staying power—even if a given integration points to a new release, the franchise associated with the release can provide value beyond the relatively tight window of alignment around a new movie studio release (or other comparable). Games tend to be played for upwards of hundreds of hours, meaning that the resonance of the game experience relative to the duration of a movie or TV show is quite high. Psychological priming for positive associations between the entertainment experience and integration can conceivably be extended far beyond the window of other, more traditional forms of media. Second, game IP will resonate more deeply with the gaming audience, and based upon our review of

89

Getting in the Game (without Changing It)

gaming as a participatory culture and form of media earlier, potentially deeper than other IP. As with all things in the gaming sector this carries advantages and disadvantages—both the credibility of the partner and the game become intimately tied, lending to the potential for both higher consumer awareness and scrutiny.[10]

Finally, these types of integrations have the benefit of potentially offering incentives not entirely unlike direct advertisements within the game environments. Whether it's redeemable for purchase of a product via codes (a popular route for consumer product goods) or performing some other action, a higher-value incentive can be attached to the integration given the potential higher-yield for the action asked of the consumer (i.e., buying a product). This in turn allows for incentive-based partnerships even amongst nonmobile games with a more limited economy, inclusive of offering durables such as skins or other "cosmetic" items at the higher end of potential values, thereby opening the possibility of business integrations with almost any genre of game on any platform (assuming alignment with the developer and a player base aligned with the interest/targeted audience for the partner). It has occasionally been the case that logoed cosmetics in game environments have been offered, though the break in process models via the presence of brand logos in a game coupled with more prohibitive development resources to facilitate these requests would position such activations as ones that should only be done with considerable care (and almost certainly at considerably more cost from the game developer).

The scope of potential games and audiences aligned with IP partnerships is more flexible than running ads directly, though it requires coordination with the game studio. In-game sponsorships take this a step further by also often requiring customized development resources on behalf of the game studio. The natural implication is both more time and costs than either direct advertisements or broader IP partnerships, but with the advantage of potentially yielding the best of both words by means of deeply leveraging an immersive game environment, in a player-forward way, across a broader swath of genres and game types (including in some cases, those on PCs or consoles).

In-game sponsorships can therefore be defined as a customized, deep in-game integration of a partner into the game environment, facilitated by the game developer. This can range from a takeover of the loading screen (which may be as simple as a logo-slap on behalf of the partner before a player enters the environment), to manifest alterations to the core game by merit of new levels, characters, or other content being developed specifically for the purposes of the partnership. Like more traditional advertising in games, in-game sponsorships can be traced back decades—in this case to the early 1990s, where the offbeat driving game *Crazy Taxi* tasked players with taking fares to Pizza Hut & KFC locations in the game world.[11] More recently players might find themselves behind the wheel of a Mercedes-Benz in *Mario Kart*,[12] playing as a Marvel superhero or NFL player in *Fortnite*,[13] or be aided by Buzz the Bee of Cheerios fame in *Angry Birds*.[14]

The potential for what can be integrated within a game is as limitless and customized as the imagination, at least in theory. In practice, a number of philosophical and logistical hurdles will come to bear—first and foremost, whether a developer is interested in outside alliances, and secondary to that the extent to which there is potential mismatch between a given outside partner and a game. For example, a car brand in a racing game isn't a far jump, but a car brand in (say) a fantasy role-playing game would create a number of issues (though a car might be a more convenient form of transportation than a horse). Some game environments such as *Fortnite* have allowed for a bafflingly large array of partner IP to appear in game, as the absurdist and cartoony nature of the game allows for just about anything to appear in game without too much distortion (after all, this was a game that heavily featured "Loot Llamas" or player skins where you could appear as having a hamburger head).

If the possibilities seem quite broad and undefined and the roadmap murky, it is because that is exactly the case. Most major game publishers will have a partnerships or alliance team that can be contacted to start the process, but the meat of what is or is not possible and overall opportunity space will largely come from discussions directly with the game studios. While we do not focus on game development within this book, excellent accounts can be found that are both accessible and entertaining to read[15] for those wishing to have a better POV on the conflicting demands and wants of game development. For now it's important to understand that game development is very different from other software development due to:[16]

- A unique combination of art and science, where artists and software engineers often have to work hand in hand.
- The sometimes fleeting nature of solving one of the seminal questions in game development: Is this experience fun?
- A lack of shared tools, protocols, or realistically much of anything in the way of common languages between development studios.

Development platforms such as Unity include both turnkey monetization options in the form of ads (and indeed, can work with brands directly to insert advertisements in a variety of games utilizing the technology) in addition to smoothing over some of the highly customized nature of game development, but on the whole the creation of games is one that is both time consuming and taxing. Thus, partners should be cognizant that frivolous or not-well-thought-out asks, a generalized lack of knowledge about games, and unrealistic expectations regarding the cost (either in capital or human hours) to craft an integration in game will not be well received. The key to partnership is … partnership, and given the relative scarcity of knowledge around the broader gaming industry a little insight can potentially go a long way in brokering trust to craft a game experience that is beneficial to all parties (specifically, the three major constituents we've discussed throughout: the partner, the game studio, and the player).

In forthcoming discussions of opportunities within esports, we'll again return to the rather amorphous shape that opportunities can take at first, with the understanding that some insider knowledge can quickly refine the intangible to something more meaningful. Even given the immense flexibility that IP or in-game sponsorships and partnerships afford, if barriers around existing games or game franchises are too daunting, the ultimate freedom in game integrations can come in the form of creating a game specifically to the goal of promoting a given message.

Branding Play: Gamevertising/Advergaming and Playables

Feel like stepping more directly into the wild world of gaming? There is hardly a better crash course than involvement in game development in a more manifest way, though the challenges present in game development are almost as numerous as the freedoms afforded.

For our purposes we'll stick with the "advergaming" nomenclature to describe games that don't just heavily feature brand promotions or are designed with capabilities for outside sponsorships and advertising to be integrated, but a game developed specifically for a brand. The earliest example of such a game is arguably the arcade hit *Tapper* in 1983, which featured prominent Budweiser branding in the background for its patron brand. The fact that one can honestly describe this game as a "hit" (it was originally designed to be featured solely in bars, but became so popular that regular arcades bought the units—though the developer switched the beverage to root beer) serves to demonstrate that advergames need not be thin marketing ploys.[17] With the right developer, these executions can be successful games in their own right.

For example, the *Chex Quest* game in 1996 on behalf of Chex cereal cribbed heavily from the massively popular game *DOOM*, but with much more family-friendly imagery (and had the advantage of being free). Around the same time, soft drink brand 7-Up made a big splash by partnering with a variety of games by software developer Virgin,[18] which the author (who was a prime demographic for both the game and soft drinks at the time) fondly remembers as being quite high-quality games. More recently, KFC adapted their tongue-in-cheek approach to marketing and relative savviness in the gaming ecosystem (how else might one dream up a game console that doubled as a chicken warmer?[19]) by releasing the anime dating-sim-inspired *I Love You Colonel Sanders,* where the player endeavors to win the heart of the ubiquitous mascot (yes, really).[20]

But does a good game make a good marketing vehicle? One might argue that one of the most successful parts of the examples above is that it's easy to forget that what one is playing is, essentially, a commercial. Some studies have shown that advergames create affinities for brands that are at least on par with television commercials.[21] Examples such as *Chex Quest* or 7-Up allegedly translated to retail sales, but whether these sales were as efficient as (say) merely running ads (or a sponsorship) is not entirely clear. The process of game development is expensive, long, and complicated. Platforms such as *Roblox* allow for lighter-weight ways in which game experiences or other virtual spaces custom-fit for brands can be created by making games within the larger *Roblox* game/framework, which are closer to a true advergame than a more baseline integration. Moreover, as game or integrations become more common (including around the concept of the metaverse), it's entirely likely that boutique development organizations who specifically focus on this type of execution will become more common and will streamline the processes to some extent.

The net result is that the creation of an advergame presents the largest amount of control for an outside partner, but also the largest liability. All the best intentions and product fit in the world can still produce something that is fundamentally not fun,[22] and therefore potentially have the opposite effect of whatever the stated goal of the strategy was intended to be. The more lightweight and accessible way to move in the direction of advergaming is presented in the form of "playable" advertisements. Unlike advertising strategies noted above, which were principally concerned with using games as platforms to showcase otherwise standard video or static ads one might see on other digital properties, a playable advertisement is one that includes an interactive element like a game but serves as a regular ad in any number of environments (though often most naturally within another game).

Playables can exist as stand-alone ad units (even outside of a game environment), or "end cards" attached to the end of a more standard video ad to increase overall engagement. In either case, not entirely unlike the baseline logic of advergames, by drawing a consumer into the advertising experience via game play the intention is to leverage the high degree of attention and mental focus directed at gaming to increase the resonance of partnership messaging. While the overall development and "fun" burden is lower than a full-fledged advergame, they are not absent—after all, someone is unlikely to interact with something if the experience is not worth interacting with.

In either case, executions that lean towards making game experiences require a high degree of expertise that most prospective businesses wishing to integrate with gaming will almost certainly lack. This similarly necessitates working with outside partners, and often

Getting in the Game (without Changing It)

those with experience in game development—an increasingly array of boutique game studios can provide a way to jump start this process. Similar to sponsorships integrations above, having some degree of know-how about the constraints and challenges of game development will inevitably ease interactions, though the partner will be in a position to give much wider direction in the case of advergaming. While freeing, this yields a classic "be careful what you wish for" scenario—a fun and worthwhile experience is subjective and challenging to weave in the best conditions, let alone one that has an ulterior motive of promoting an exogenous business proposition, and few game developers will describe the process of making a game as anything but abjectly painful.

Setting the Difficulty Level: Conclusions

The modern era of gaming is one that includes the broadest range of monetization options for game studios to offset the historically high costs associated with game development. This has presented a number of opportunities for studios to diversify their thinking around how to transact with customers, and in doing so has opened the door for integrations with outside businesses. However, just because the door has been opened, it need not be kicked in—the unique attachment individuals have to games, and the delicate cognitive processes that are evoked in affective gameplay are easily disrupted by incongruous elements. Interested partners should be wary of being too heavy handed, as game studios almost certainly already are.

The net result is an array of potential opportunities within the gaming landscape that carry a variety of considerations ranging across a number of axes including required monetary investment, time investment, player disruptiveness, and potential for resonance. As such, while the potential opportunities in gaming are wide, the right fit for a given strategy may be more limited based upon these factors. The broad categories outlined above can thus be summarized as in Table 5.1.

Table 5.1 Broad Categories of Opportunities in Gaming

	Advertisements	Partnerships	Advergaming
Monetary Investment	*Low*	*Moderate to High*	*High*
Time Investment	*Low*	*Moderate to High*	*High*
Game Studio Coordination	*Low*	*Moderate to High*	*High*
Player Disruptiveness	*Low to Moderate*: free-to-play games have more breathing room relative to games with upfront transactions.	*Low to Moderate*: pending thematic fit with the game and studio orientation to weaving in outside messaging.	*Low*: Presumably the player knows what they are in for when playing one of these games, though as noted a bad game is a bad game whether it's an advergame or not. The potential for making a bad game experience that detracts from larger brand equity is thus quite high.
Resonance	*Low to Moderate*: with incentivized and intrinsic in-play advertising being more effective than forced or interstitial executions.	*Moderate to High*: here too, depending on thematic resonance and whether incentivized elements can be included.	*Low to High*: a good game is a good game whether it's an advergame or not: There is evidence that the potential for brand impact via game play can be quite effective, and a good game can therefore be an effective vehicle for interested entities.

Getting in the Game (without Changing It)

Given the array of options, where to start? Here too, it depends: As noted, many game studios have partnership organizations that can talk through the full funnel of opportunities noted above, such as game platforms or various in-game advertising technology companies. One can even get started by simply buying game inventory through popular supply sources like Google. Ideally, leveraging the more direct expertise that a partnerships arm of a game studio can provide will alleviate some of the more common roadblocks to a successful integration, in addition to closer coordination with the game studio, albeit with the disadvantage of only addressing a smaller potential universe of game titles (those within the portfolio of the studio).

One way or another, integrating with gaming has never been easier, or more advantageous. Whether it's directly connected with a studio or through an advertising exchange, the basic rules of how to best integrate largely remain the same, and much of this logic lends itself to understanding game environments and how players interact with them. The near-term value of these lessons can be applied almost immediately; in a more future-looking world such as the metaverse, it's entirely likely that the same general rules apply. Virtual avatars holding virtual products, or emblazoned with advertisements, have already been studied and found to tangibly motivate consumers opinions' around brands.[23] As a result, the work done now to understand and interact with the gaming ecosystem has the potential to pay dividends into future strategic thinking more broadly concerned with virtual worlds that exist outside of the domain of gaming. A smart approach to gaming is thus not just a good idea; it's an ongoing strategic advantage.

Part II

Watching the Game: Esports, Streaming, and Games as a Viewing Experience

Chapter 6

Multiplayer

An Introduction to Esports

G aming in the more general sense has almost always been a social endeavor, and one where the socialization was shaped by competition. Some of the earliest known games, dating back as far as thousands of years ago, generally revolved around the concept of capturing game pieces from an opponent.[1] The first commercially successful electronic game, *Pong*, was likewise a competition between opponents. And while some of the most popular games to follow would occasionally pit the player against a computerized opponent, recorded high scores on these machines allowed for human opponents to measure themselves against each other in an asynchronous way. Importantly, the proliferation of arcade games in the 1970s introduced the norm of spectating video game play— teens would huddle around machines to compare skills while putting down a quarter to claim who was next in line.

In short, one shouldn't be terribly surprised that the professionalization of competitive video games, colloquially known as *esports*, has become a worldwide phenomenon. It was a bit of an inevitability— witnessing high levels of skill in any given endeavor is interesting in and of itself, but potentially more so when it is an area of personal interest. As video gaming becomes increasingly ensconced in popular culture, the interest in demonstrations of skill at the highest levels followed. The ludicrousness of the mere prospect of playing video games for a money became a fixation of popular media, occasionally buzzing in and out at the tentpole moments of a larger and complex history.

And yet for every (typically older) person who gives a light-hearted chuckle at the headlines outlining million-dollar prize pools with a dry joke that they should get into gaming (or more likely, have their kids game more), there looms the larger reality that these million-dollar prizes and larger commercial successes are exceedingly rare. There are billions of gaming fans out there and yet only a few thousand will ever make much money professionally—even fewer enough money to live on. The flow of money into esports is significantly more unpredictable than comparable media outlets or competitive endeavors (those you might consider "legitimate" sports or otherwise).

As a result, the formalized *business* of competitive gaming is reasonably new and occasionally unstable. At the onset, few got into professional gaming to get rich, but as the eyeballs accumulated, the opportunity scaled. The more that the industry scaled, the further it found itself from the grassroots passion-led tactics it was built on. The word "passion" is used a lot in the description of esports, particularly as a means to describe what makes the industry a special stand-out among more traditional sports or competitive entertainment offerings (and indeed, we'll get into whether or not "esports" are truly a "sport").

Depending on your vantage point, "passion" can easily be seen as a code word for naivete. While to many the word "esports" represents a new type of media filled with exciting professional opportunities, to others it's little more than a more structured way for folks to waste time—yet another path along which younger generations have lost their way instead of getting "real" jobs. The constant articulation of passion is not only a defining attribute of the fans and evangelists, but for many years that's all the entire industry had to run on.

The modern esports industry is experiencing growing pains. The patchwork scaffolding of the early business is slowly being replaced with enduring structures. More directly, the industry is in the midst of the hard work of translating from a bedroom operation to a board-room one. And for all the worries of the industry operating as a bubble about to burst, one must recognize the fact that it is an industry built on an *already* burst bubble.

Perhaps somewhat obviously, this is not without tension. It's an industry that strives for stable revenue and legitimization in popular culture, and often finds both in the form of outside investment (particularly from blue chip brands or legacy sporting organizations). Yet there are concerns that the outside business interests and professionals carrying through such deals are overriding and stomping out the grassroots community. The misunderstandings on either side of this divide are quite high, and intentions are equally mixed. Passion alone certainly won't build the industry, but neither will applications of business practices that don't understand or respect what makes this form of media unique.

Nonetheless, esports is one of the most exciting and attractive sectors of the larger gaming ecosystem, albeit with a heavy dose of hyperbole. As you might glean from the account above, we will lean towards objective judgment as much as possible—outlining opportunity while acknowledging that the industry is very much in the process of finding its footing among larger cultural, societal, and business pillars.

So, what is esports? It's passion. It's competition. It's hype. It's a tug-of-war between grassroots fans and business folks. It's the expression of generations looking to legitimize and capitalize on their pastime. It's the complex weave of opportunity tempered by very real business challenges. It's emerging, yet it has a history dating back at least 50 years. It's worth your time and attention, because in many respects it has evolved beyond simply emulating traditional sports frameworks to pioneering a framework for commercialization that more traditional sports are emulating. Whether or not you buy into the concept of professionalized and competitive video gaming in the general sense (though you should!), it is nonetheless (one way or another) the future of competitive entertainment.

Watching Games, Together

To many outside the industry, the emergence of esports as a cultural phenomenon seemingly happened overnight. As noted above, the history of esports can be traced back at least 50 years—so why the sudden hype? The following chapter provides a more thorough overview of the essential history of esports—for now, the important takeaway is that the seemingly sudden rise of esports is (like so many other phenomena in modern business) due to the internet, and those darn kids (though maybe not in the way you might think).

Competitive gaming as an industry or personal endeavor was previously quite localized—the internet allowed the competitive landscape to evolve from a given city or block to essentially the entire world. Network effects across various games, chat platforms, social media, or other venues allowed smaller individual groupings to develop into a massive audience. Competitive gaming took root culturally and socially at much higher rates within regions where high-speed internet is readily available (the exemplar being South Korea). In essence, it was raised to the level of media, meaning the apparent opportunity was clearer to a larger group of potentially interest parties.

The potential to scale a previously niche audience is of particular importance to esports because it (like gaming) is incredibly fragmented. The modern esports industry can be described as a rough assembly of dozens of game publishers, game titles, competitive teams, league structures, tournament series, technological platforms, and partnering institutions (both endemic and nonendemic). Saying you are an esports fan is not more specific than saying you are a sports fan. Esports fans can therefore be fans of a particular team, individual, genre, publisher, a tournament, or some combination of the above. Though the esports industry has, at various times and in various spaces, attempted to structure itself in ways that are similar to more traditional sports (including localized teams to foster regional affinities or loyalties among fans), the makeup of the fandom is profoundly diversified. With a few notable exceptions we will discuss here, the industry is entirely reliant upon unifying a dispersed audience via the internet, not only because distribution through traditional media channels is problematic, but to capitalize on the endlessly diverse pockets of the fandom.

The eventuality of competitive gaming becoming mainstream is, like gaming, woven into generational patterns (or depending on your POV, experiential patterns). The most salient reference point comes from classic psychology in the form of the "mere exposure" effect.[2] Intuitively, the effect represents the idea that we are more comfortable with an experience that we've had before, rather than a new one. Younger generations are both more likely to play games and have more balanced feelings about the impact of games on negative connotations such as real-world violence.[3] Put simply, we either fear or misunderstand the unknown, and gaming both as a pastime and a vocation tends to be proportionally less known by older populations but is well within the comfort zone of those exposed to gaming throughout their lives. As discussed before, now-adult generations have grown up gaming, and affinity for the pastimes of youth such as video games has increasingly been carried forward to the heads of modern households.

Much in the way that gaming more generally has been increasingly socialized as being a "normal" or "non-fringe" media activity, so increasingly goes the concept of watching someone else play a videogame. The gaming research firm Newzoo estimates that global viewership of games being livestreamed will reach 921.2 million by the end of 2022, and will be in excess of 1.4 billion by 2025. Esports viewership is estimated to reach 532 million by the end of 2022, and reach upwards of 640.8 million by 2025.[4]

But even if esports are familiar and have a growing fan base, why watch at all? Esports, like more traditional sports, have the same features that tend to drive audiences: competitive stakes, drama, and unknown outcomes are universal motivators for viewership among virtually any formalized competition. Above and beyond these commonalities, esports are unique insofar that they are a place of community on what was the fringes of popular culture, one where spectatorship and participation are intimately linked—virtually all spectators of a given esport tend to be players of the game in question, and improving their own skill drives engagement. Sure, I'd wager that most NFL fans have played football at some point in their life, but how many of them are doing so on a daily basis? Not many, and the extent to which practice, play, and viewership are intermingled in the majority of esports fandom is both a key point of differentiation and driver for the uniquely high levels of fan engagement that are common within esports.

However, the question has officially been begged—is this a fair comparison when it's not clear that esports are an actual sport? One of the most fundamental questions leveled at esports among those seeking to understand the space has the fundamentally flaw of not really mattering all that much.

Defining Esports: Are They More E or More Sport?

More traditional sports have had the benefit of being ingrained within popular culture for, at times, hundreds of years. While the history of esports is quite a bit longer than most would expect, we're still only talking about a handful of decades. The newness of esports therefore makes it equally exciting and confusing to the uninitiated.

The games that are successful as esports have several commonalities fundamental to competition: one or more persons facing off within a set field, with defined rules and goals, and a clear winner. This can range from which team eliminates the other with gunplay, scores a goal, or wins a card game. Put simply, a game where an esports community can potentially calcify is often designed with the intent to pit human components against one another. While there are ways in which individually oriented games have been turned into a competitive platform (a phenomenon we will discuss more in the chapter on streaming), the first key component is that it is a PVP (player vs. player) vs. a PVE (player vs. environment—i.e. a level, game AI, etc.) challenge.

Above and beyond the competitive aspect, esports industry fixture William Collis notes that the most successful titles are those that are:[5]

- **Viewable:** Can be watched/understood easily, though this is far from a given and a particularly acute challenge in esports, which we will unpack.
- **Uncertain:** Implementations of chance as a mechanism to increase drama and tension in what could otherwise be a machine-perfect execution in a virtual environment.
- **Skill-based:** Put simply, there is a high degree of differentiation between good and bad players.
- **Transferable:** The skills required to play the game can be applied to others in a similar genre.

A consequence of the rise of esports as a revenue-generating vehicle has spurred the development of titles that were essentially built to be good vehicles for professional play and therefore tick most of the above boxes. A recent example would be Riot Game's *Valorant*, which essentially smashed two of the most popular competitive first-person shooter (FPS) titles in the form of *Counter Strike: Global Offensive* and *Overwatch* together. That said, many of the most popular esports titles were not necessarily designed to be esports, and some others have roots via fan modifications within the broader gaming community. While much in the esports industry will intrinsically be controlled by the game publishers (either directly through esports outreach or indirectly through control of the game titles), the extent to which the fandom has had (and will likely continue to have) an influence on the core structure of the industry is a unique artifact of the modern and connected age.

The constant reference to community and community adoption is deliberate—no person or entity can declare on high that a game title should become part of the esport ecosystem. It is certainly the case that publishers have fostered a competitive community via the creation of a formalized "league," but such formalization was predicated by the title having a large fan base. In other (less happy) cases, the game publisher might be semi-hostile to the competitive community built around a given game (with the evergreen example being Nintendo with respect to their *Smash Bros.* series of fighting games, which only very recently started to become more accommodating to formalized competition),[6] yet a competitive community still thrives.

At the highest levels, players can be entirely professionalized in their game play, thereby often spending hundreds of hours practicing and honing their craft. The route to professionalism is, like fandom itself, fragmented yet occasionally exceedingly elegant—most esports titles include competitive "ladders" upon which any given player can assess their skill and relative ranking against others within the game. The best are, quite literally, at the top of the game. More traditional paths to professional play (high school teams, to college, to pro, etc.) are becoming more common, with hundreds of high schools[7] and colleges[8] developing esports teams that mirror the format of professional play.

Professional-level play requires an intense amount of strategic thinking, teamwork, practice, and dedication. It is not surprising, as a result, to see that traditional professional sports players tend to over-index as individuals that play games. This isn't simply because they are within the demographic that plays games more heavily (young males, classically), but rather much of the same mentality and personality traits that allow one to thrive in a competitive physical environment translate to a virtual environment. And while mindset is perhaps the most important and defining feature of a professional who competes in a virtual environment, like traditional sports there is a high degree of differential physicality required to be the best of the best.

It's right about here that I suspect the esports cynics are raising an eyebrow. Playing a game is physical? Yes, and moreover, as is the case in traditional sports, the highest-performing esports professionals are often physically gifted above and beyond most folks. A recent study has shown that the reaction time of an esports player is not entirely different from a more traditional athlete, and in many cases superior (and both were significantly faster than the control).[9] Games such as *Starcraft II*, which require immense and highly complicated strategizing around the economies and development of an army to defeat an opponent, also require lightning-fast capabilities to input commands at the highest level. Measured in actions per minute (APM), an amateur or causal player might register 60–100 (which, to be clear, still represents one or two commands in game every second) whereas professionals are often within the 300–600 range (upwards of 10 actions every second—try hitting even a single key on your keyboard 10 times in a second, to get an idea of just how fast those commands are inputted).

The defining physicality of esports is thus one of control over the technological interface that the player interacts within. Traditional sports are defined by the laws of physics, whereas esports often entail in-game avatars untethered from the rules of reality. This occasionally includes pros assuming the same avatar with the same abilities—ostensibly a great equalizer in gaming—everyone can have the same abilities to move and manipulate the competitive space in the same way. The esports professional is simply "piloting" one of these avatars at a high level. While it is fair to argue that the kind of physicality required to (say) pilot an FPS avatar at a high level is quite a bit different from what is required for a good jump shot, physical control of the keyboard, mouse, or controller, with lightning-quick reaction times are a defining aspect of pro players.

This level of differentiated physicality, combined with a knowledge of the game or game environment to an extent that moves, feints, and actions take place in a spectrum that nonprofessionals cannot see represents the key differentiator between someone "just playing a game" and an "esports professional" or "athlete." Here again—is having differentially good knowledge, strategic thinking, and technological control enough to warrant the label of "athletes" within a "sport?" While all of the above are performed through skilled manipulation of a technological layer, what are sports such as cycling or F1 if not technologically moderated competitions?[10] The appearance of these pros may not carry the same aesthetic beauty as a runner or gymnast (I'll be blunt—esports pros often conform quite well with the mental image one might conjure when asked to think about a "gaming nerd"), but one doesn't have to look far in more established "traditional" sports such as bowling or baseball to see similarly shaped and sized bodies.

We will not put an end to this debate here; even within the esports community there are proponents of considering it a sport—or not. On a more official basis, the International Olympics Committee has opened a series of forums since at least 2018 as to whether esports should be a medaled event[11] (leaving aside how one picks which game or games would be representative, which will almost certainly become a sticky problem). For our purposes, we'll return to the point this section opened with: it should not matter much to business decision makers. At most, the status of "sport or not" raises tactical concerns as to where esports should fit into traditional budgets. Whether esports are legitimized as a sport or not, fans are watching in droves.

A (slightly) less cynical take on the argument would be that officiating of a "sport" is important insofar as it lends legitimacy. The legitimacy of esports, particularly in reference to the sports world by means of common business practices within, represents one of the most fundamental challenges with the industry at large.

Ready? Fight: Challenges and Considerations

As a rapidly developing industry, esports are not without a number of challenges, some of which are those that one might expect with any developing media format; others are unique to the peculiarities of the industry. We'll concentrate on three of the most salient ones to outside partners: business practices, viewership, and representation.

The business of esports is still relatively nascent—as relative interest within the industry increased and the operations within became more sophisticated, the early grassroots fans found themselves rubbing elbows with professionals from traditional sports. The trend was simple enough—as noted, much of the more formalized aspects within esports has looked to the traditional sports model. The reasoning then became that these traditional sports professionals would be able to uplift the business practices of esports to propel the industry towards similar levels of financial success that more traditional sports offerings enjoy. Moreover, the core draw of esports is that it is increasingly the domain of a very difficult to reach demographic: 20-something males who don't consume large amounts of linear television. Much in the same way that the NFL overtook the MLB in the transition from radio to television, the coming digital age portends a world where (in the eyes of entrepreneurial and forward-thinking sports execs) esports would overtake more traditional sports while yielding audiences that the businesses are very much seeking.

Unfortunately, this book hasn't existed until now, and many of the traditional sports execs didn't really have an avenue to gain an understanding of the broader esports industry. Given the high regard for authenticity among esports fans and grassroots founders, who at times were all but doing "community service" to keep the industry alive,[12] there have been some natural frictions in terms of how to take esports to the next level.[13]

One of the most hotly contested debates in this tug-of-war is one of the challenges proposed above: viewership. Many of the strategies for traditional sports relies upon the massive fan bases those sports command—and while esports fandom is growing at an impressive rate, it's not quite at the level of traditional sports. As a result, the same sales pitches that might have been successful for (say) the NFL don't really resonate when you swap out cleats for magic staves. Similarly, increasingly viewership remains a challenge insofar that the barriers to fandom are quite a bit higher than they are for traditional sports—even if you don't understand the rules, just about everyone who has been exposed to baseball can likely understand the fundamental idea. This is absolutely not the case for a games like *Overwatch* or *League of Legends*, which require tremendous viewing (and, likely, playing) experience to understand even the most basic dynamics within the game.

Make no mistake, based in part on the factors discussed above (e.g., generational effects, increased educational uptake of esports) it's extremely likely that various esports titles will scale to the size of more traditional sports. However, that time is not now, and as a result the core business entities have needed to look at a wide array of strategies and revenue opportunities to keep the industry in the black (we'll discuss these over the next few chapters). Until these broader mechanisms for funneling new fans into the industry are fully developed, the fandom (and to an extent, the professionals within the industry) remain in a fairly narrow demographic band. This is one of the value propositions that esports has to offer partners, but it also carries the unfortunate side effect where broader representation is an issue.

Specifically, because esports fandom relies heavily upon experience playing the games in question, and these games are overwhelmingly PC titles, the fandom is overwhelmingly populated with more "hardcore" gaming enthusiasts. As a practical illustration, one of the most popular esports in the world happens to be played within a game that is the poster child for toxicity in gaming: *League of Legends*. These same enthusiasts tend to be the same that propagate toxicity and gatekeeping behaviors within gaming more generally, in addition to being largely upper-middle-class, white, male, and young. The result is an industry and fandom that is exclusionary, and fans or professionals who are women and/or minorities are relatively rare. The same early-days grassroots fans and organizers of esports who have directed exclusionary efforts towards the incoming wave of sports execs occasionally do the same towards underrepresented groups such as women looking to make a foothold within the industry. When esports tournament organizer ESL proposed a women's league for popular FPS *Counter Strike: Global Offensive*,[14] many longtime and prominent voices in the broader esports industry questioned the necessity and precedent that this move set.

An interesting and partial exception to the narrowness of representation in esports is the fighting game community (FGC). As a genre, fighting games usually involve two players attacking one another with a series of punches or kicks (often in the form of traditional martial arts, sometimes not) until the health of an opponent is depleted enough to "knock them out." Popularized by games such as *Street Fighter II*, fighting games and FGC have deep roots in arcades. By some accounts, *Street Fighter II* is the third-highest-grossing arcade machine (just behind *Pac-Man* and *Space Invaders*), pulling in ~$2.3 billion in revenue across ~200,000 arcade cabinets.[15] Arcade machines present a significantly lower barrier of entry than a game-ready PC (as little as a quarter is all that is needed to play), and as a result the FGC is significantly more diverse and tends to lean more urban than PC-based esports do. However, in part because the Japanese companies that produce fighting games (notably, Capcom and Nintendo) have been relatively reluctant to invest in competitive tournaments around their products,[16] the FGC has remained significantly more grassroots and mistrusting of corporate influence relative to their PC-based colleagues.[17] Ironically, this contributes to the lack of representation in esports as the most diverse of the competitive gaming communities simply do not identify with the label of "esports."

Shaping the Meta: Conclusions and Implications

Good competitive entertainment requires drama and stakes. Esports certainly have their fair share, and not simply in the form of competition; it extends to the core businesses encompassing the wider industry. Competitive gaming, and the broader phenomena of fans watching gaming, presents a unique window into the future of media consumption and how the audience and content producer interact, in addition to expectations among fans to be more deeply involved with the content they watch. The passionate fan base and highly affective nature of the content present a unique way to interact with audiences, but one in which a high degree of care should be taken not to run afoul of the challenges within the industry or conflicts with the fan base.

We'll follow this brief introduction to esports with a series of chapters to give the proper background and context to interested marketers and executives, starting with a brief history of esports that outlines core tensions relating to growing a grassroots movement into the domain of big business, including finding the proper medium for esports to thrive—online streaming. We'll turn to the generalized world of game streaming since the overlap between these two industries bears consideration, particularly as partnering with streamers or streaming platforms becomes an increasingly attractive and accessible way for partners to integrate into gaming. Having covered the necessary background we'll dive into a primer on opportunities for integration within the world of esports and streaming. As has been the case in opportunities within gaming, the idea is not to provide an exhaustive list and how-to of tactics, but rather to provide a map to navigate these spaces and understand the relative strengths and weaknesses of any given entry point.

It's fairly well accepted that, intuitively, gaming is fun. Who knew that watching someone play games could be just as much fun (hint: apparently millions of people; let's learn a bit more about them)?

Chapter 7

Good Luck Having Fun

The Rise of Esports

The beginning of esports is less well agreed-upon than the proper casing (to be clear, it is "esports," lowercase) but not quite as contentious as the debate around whether it is a sport. Some have argued that the origination date is closer to 1942, when pinball machines with flippers (i.e., human skill) were introduced.[1] While we'll rely on the more conventionally accepted start at the 1972 *Spacewars!* tournament at Stanford University, this still represents a considerable span of time for the development of a phenomenon that most view as only recently emergent. Like many new forms of media, extreme levels of hype were soon to follow—depending on the headlines one reads or the pundits one believes, you're equally likely to evaluate esports as the biggest opportunity in business, or mere puffery. As with so many things, the truth is somewhere in between, and more structured views of its evolution are the first necessary steps towards a more informed, and less hyperbolic, view.

Much like our foray into the history of gaming, our purpose here is not an exhaustive history so much as identifying the pivotal and business-critical moments that propelled the phenomenon of esports towards the wider cultural acceptance it enjoys today. Along the way, our focus will be less an exhaustive accounting of every pivotal business deal, team, or personality, so much as extracting broader meaning applicable to how one should view and integrate with this space, in addition to lessons for the business world beyond esports. What follows is what some might consider a surprisingly complex history that paints a picture of old media formats (such as broadcast TV) struggling to capture the inherently interactive mediums such as gaming, and an industry that has only truly found footing in the era of networked game play and user-generated content.

Not entirely unlike gaming, the rise of esports is a story of balancing economic realities against formalizing an audience, though the journey here is on a different trajectory from that of gaming more generally. From its roots in more traditional gaming formats, esports as an industry has spent less time on how to appeal to the masses (e.g., through casual gaming) so much as massifying what is, at this time, a more narrowly defined yet incredibly fragmented fan base. Esports came to prominence with the ubiquity of user-generated content—not just as a better distribution channel for the official matches, but as a means through which the entities in the space found economic and business models that allowed for stability outside of tournament winnings, and a means to unite a fandom across dozens of different games, tournaments, and leagues.

If the rise of gaming was about finding ways to weave it into the lives of everyone, the rise of esports is about how modern forms of entertainment find footing and legitimacy outside the bounds of legacy media. Gaming and esports as marketing opportunities have quickly gained the attention of business decision makers in recent years not simply because of their relative "newness" (as indeed, both have been around for quite some time), but the ways in which they've become entrenched and part of the everyday media ecosystem of an emerging cohort of household decision makers. Understanding esports is less about coming to terms with why someone might enjoy watching a video game being played, so much as a lens through which one can understand the future of professionalized competition.

In this respect, understanding the cultural and technological roots of the current state of esports is a filter to separate the considerable hype surrounding the industry from fact. Misunderstandings and misevaluations (positive or negative) as they pertain to esports often come from a position devoid of knowledge around the grassroots history and early struggles of this industry. This is understandable to some extent, as despite all the enthusiasm around esports today, it is an industry that largely developed below the radar of popular culture and media for decades.

This leaves quite a bit of unfamiliar ground to cover. To make the task at hand a bit more manageable, not entirely unlike the previously described history of gaming, we'll segment this history into a series of chronological eras. Each era is divided not by fixed intervals of time so much as by moments in the history of the medium that signal larger shifts within the industry. For the sake of simplicity, we'll largely focus on the Western esports scene with occasional trips overseas to Korea:

- **The Novelty Era (~1972–1996):** The period through which the first legitimate esports competitions were structured, resulting in an assemblage of more or less regulated competitions around various platforms, often utilized principally as a form of marketing for the core games, which can be credited with socializing video games in popular culture from a frivolous novelty towards a more serious competitive endeavor.

- **The Online Era (~1997–2008):** Esports truly found a footing with the proliferation of the consumer internet, though seemingly lost its way (and nearly everything) after a sojourn to Hollywood for the brief renaissance of esports on linear TV. We'll make our first stop in Korea here, to get a sense of a society where esports were more fully embraced by popular culture.

Good Luck Having Fun

From rapid growth to full-industry crash, this period represents one where lessons of how outside businesses and structures can influence esports in equally negative and positive ways were hard-learned.

- **The Networked Era (2009–2015):** Esports found a home in a truly global and digital-native world. With the launch of Twitch in 2011, the media of esports found a medium across which it could proliferate at a rate, scale, and format that legacy media distributions could not afford. The heavy influence of the esports community comes back to light during this time, where game modders set the foundation for one of the most influential genres in esports.

- **The Content Era (2016–Now):** The foundation of major governing league structures attempted to craft more points of comparison between traditional sports and esports. In tandem with this development, individual actors and organizations across these structured lines of competitive play are shifting towards the business of lifestyle content creation as a major form of commercialization. Between these two forces is a proliferation of corporate alliances where legitimization of esports by "blue chip" brands is increasingly being traded for the attention and relevance of audiences that are difficult to reach by more traditional means.

Each of these eras can be understood as a set of particular moments defined by the overlapping influence of the cultural relevance of gaming (increasingly across the years), the commercialization structures that esports relied upon (diversifying and differentiating across the years), and the mediums through which the media is consumed (becoming more specialized across the years). What do not define these eras (for the most part) are interventions from outside cash infusions or venture capital—it should be understood that while esports have occasionally commanded large streams of funding, any particular boost or bubble was largely the result of technological or cultural barriers (or lack thereof) creating more or less direct pathways for competitive gaming to rise to the level of acceptance within larger society.

The Novelty Era of Esports (~1972–1996)

The Novelty Era of esports represents a series of semi-structured but often ad hoc competitions structured around competitive gaming, where many of the modern artifacts of what was to become the esports industry were grounded—even down to how serious competitors played these games.

From the *Spacewars!* competition at Stanford in 1972, formalized competition in video gaming was sporadic and manifested as only a few notable entries. Nearly a decade later, in 1980, Atari created the Space Invaders Championship, banking off the wild success of the tournament's namesake game. This represents one of the first formalized tournaments where a game developer created and hosted the structure of competition. It would not be the last—as we'll see, esports have necessarily existed in the gravitational pull of the very game publishers that created the games, with varying degrees of intensity and investment.

Nintendo is a perfect example of this undulation, ranging from being a pivotal participant in early esports to sporadic involvement in more recent years. The 1984 Nintendo World Championship was a video game tournament at a scale never before reached in the industry. For nine months across 29 cities, more than 8,000 players accumulated (in hindsight, somewhat illogical) aggregated scores across a number of Nintendo titles ranging from *Rad Racer* to *Super Mario Brothers 3*.[2] In addition to posting the largest prizes to date in competitive gaming (a $10,000 bond, a 40-inch TV, and a Geo Metro), the hundreds of gaming stations and outsized competitive-viewing screens were immortalized in *The Wizard* movie/multi-hour-long Nintendo ad.

Using esports as a marketing tactic for a given game (or in this case, games) is still a fairly common tactic in today's esports scene, though opportunities for businesses within these executions were still only nascent given the popular appraisal of video game tournaments as a novelty. Beyond the origins of esports as a marketing ploy, the Nintendo World Championships was one of the first large-scale tournaments that demonstrated skill in gaming matters, and is a legitimate differentiator between folks who enjoy games and those who compete at the highest level. Perhaps much to the disappointment of bemused parents everywhere, merely knowing how to hold a controller is not quite enough for their little ones to parlay their afternoon leisure time into serious money.

The impact and differentiating effect of skill is perhaps no more apparent than our final notable moment of this era, the Deathmatch 95 tournament, hosted by then gaming-fringe organization Microsoft. At the time, PCs were largely not a serious platform for gaming. Windows 95 was designed to streamline the operation and installation of a variety of software, including games. Moreover, in one of the many interweaved pivotal points between the history of gaming and esports, games like *Super Mario Bros. 3* influenced pushing the technological boundaries of early PC game development to foster smoothly scrolling textures and other mainstays present in console gaming.[3] So began the origination of legendary FPS games such as *DOOM*, the platform upon which one of the first esports superstars, Dennis "Thresh" Fong, built his fame.

Fong wasn't just *good* at games like *DOOM* and sister competitive shooter *Quake*, he was "eliminate the competition without being hit" good. He pioneered control techniques such as using the WASD keys on a keyboard to move his in-game avatar rather than the regular arrow keys to create more natural space between his keyboard and mouse hand, in addition to easier access to nearby keys to select different weapons or movements. He memorized the layout of maps and areas where various resources in the game could be obtained easily (and at what times)—in other words, he set the standard for what differentiates someone who might be "good" at a given game vs. one of the best.

This "novelty" era thus represents the transition from competition in video gaming from a mere novelty to what could be argued to be serious, legitimate competition with high degrees of differentiation in skill and knowledge being the defining factor between success and defeat. While using competitions as elaborate expressions of experiential marketing for games (or game platforms, such as Windows 95) is indeed a practice that carries into the modern era, the growing scale of these events begins to present an opportunity where the competitive aspects of gaming can be structured as independent businesses. The question becomes, how to get these businesses to the masses, and are these presumed masses ready for them?

The Online of Esports (~1997–2008)

If there was any point in your life that you had heard about a major prize in esports, it's very likely the prize of the 1997 "Red Annihilation" tournament: legendary game programmer John Carmack's Ferrari 328 GTS. Though games like *DOOM* began to popularize the concept of playing games on the internet, the telecommunications infrastructure at the time did not quite allow for a game to be seamlessly played between (say) the East and West Coasts of the United States. As a result, it was the first time that Dennis "Thresh" Fong played Tom "Entropy" Kimzey, and the result was a complete blowout victory for Fong. He took home not only the

Ferrari, but a heavy dollop of media attention given the headline-grabbing nature of the prize.

The stage was well set for the Cyberathlete Professional League (CPL) to be founded that same year on a wave of attention from these early tournaments, hosting a series of competitions through this period and one of the first attempts to structure competitive gaming in a format similar to traditional sports. In tandem with these developments, a country with more developed internet infrastructure took the concept of competitive gaming to new heights.

After being hit hard by the Asian Financial Crisis in 1997, the South Korean government turned to information technology as a widespread institutional bet for revitalizing the economy. The government invested some $11 billion into the network infrastructure of the country over the next five years. This equated to comparatively cheap high-speed internet for the majority of South Koreans. Widespread high-speed internet, combined with very concentrated populations and droves of unemployed folks seeking places outside the home to spend time, yielded the proliferation of "PC Bangs." Roughly translating to "PC Rooms," these internet cafes offered cheap eats and open licenses to a host of competitive PC games—most famously for the Koreans, this included the 1998 mega-hit *Starcraft*, where later iterations would become colloquially known as the national pastime of the country.[4]

What's notable about developments in South Korea are not just the massive tournaments, prize purses, and mega-starts such as Lim "BoxeR" Yo-hwan pioneering personal endorsement deals, but the extent to which professional gaming was normalized into the fabric of Korean society. Structural factors such as the creation of government organizations like KeSPA (Korea e-sports Association) and broadcasts on specialized TV networks via OGN (Ongamenet) cemented the importance of gaming and esports in modern South Korean culture (both among the youth and older generations).

The hard truth facing the blossoming esports industry back in the United States was that cultural acceptance, as in South Korea, is a necessary precursor to mass adoption. While prize money in esports during this period was on the rise due in part to entities such as CPL, television broadcasts of competitive gaming in the United States did not enjoy the mainstream success as those in South Korea. Quite the opposite—the stage was set for the industry to collapse.

In 2006 the "Cyber Gaming Series" (CGS) debuted on DirectTV in the United States; problems related to situating video game tournaments in a format for TV were immediately apparent. The global financial crisis essentially ended the series in 2008, after only two seasons. In doing so, the early assumptions that TV would be the vehicle through which esports was propelled to the ranks of traditional sporting events were dashed. This cancelation also served a near-fatal blow to the industry at large: Based upon the failure of CGS, corporate investment in competitive gaming dried up, and tournament prize purses were essentially halved.[5]

The actual broadcast themselves struggled to solidify even those deeply interested in esports by selecting games to showcase with broader "mass appeal" (such as *Project Gotham Racing*) than those with established competitive communities, and made production decisions that prized TV drama and aesthetics over accepted game play conventions among the community (such as shortening the number of rounds in competitive shooter *Counter-Strike*). The result was a bit of a "worst of both worlds" scenario where fans were alienated, and newcomers not yet given quite enough information to contextualize or understand the competitive stakes. The need to remain true to the fan base and deliver content in a way that was fit for the interactive nature of video games was a hard-learned lesson during this time.

While it is easy to see this era as a dark point in the narrative of esports, a number of important innovations (or in some cases, realizations) came to light. First, perhaps most notably from the seeds of the Deathmatch 95 event, the PC emerged as the most prominent platform for esports. Much of the popularity of early PC gaming was due to online-enabled games, allowing for competitive scenes to grow beyond the bounds of local events or communities. The extent to which online gaming permeated popular culture appears to be roughly commensurate with the sophistication of internet infrastructure in the given area—where esports in South Korea flourished, the United States was just finding its footing. Much of the early success in the United States was almost completely lost due to the translatability of gaming content to the TV for the presumed optimal U.S. viewing experience from producers who might not have fully understood competitive gaming to a casual audience that wasn't terribly interested.

Ultimately, understanding the trajectory of esports requires understanding cultural, societal, and technological factors around the media—both within the fandom and the larger popular culture that envelopes it. Moreover, creating a viewing experience that embraces the established community while remaining open to new fans (beyond the false hope that they will merely "flip the channel" to gaming and become fans) remains one of the biggest challenges for the industry even today. Both of these concerns found a partial solve with the proliferation of internet streaming.

The Networked Era of Esports (2009–2015)

After various forays into more generalized live "life streaming" on Justin.tv, Twitch.tv was launched in public beta in 2011 with the realization that some of the most popular content on the platform was related to gaming. Even as commercial internet became more viable for online gaming, consumption of gaming content not directly related to playing was difficult to come by (and as noted above, certainly quite scant on TV). And yet, existing mechanisms for broadcasting on the internet were either crude or expensive, creating difficulties for both individual enthusiasts and the surviving esports organizations.

Twitch provided an elegant solution to both problems while fusing in a social component to the livestream, thereby allowing for fans not just to spectate à la a linear broadcast, but mingle and chat with fellow enthusiasts while spectating. As with the proliferation of online games, being able to find more abundant community *en masse* over the internet allowed for esports producers and fans to find a media vehicle better suited for their medium than television. Twitch was not the first (or even today, only) service to cater to gaming enthusiasts—it overcame incumbents such as Ustream by merit of the fact that the core team at Twitch deeply cared about gaming. Here again, authenticity and understanding matter—in this case, the payoff was nearly cornering an emerging field of platforms.

While YouTube had for years been well utilized by the esports community to distribute game videos, the live and interactive nature of streaming sites such as Twitch provided a format that was both better fit for live content and social interactivity. In recent years YouTube has invested heavily into YouTube Gaming for livestreaming, and social media juggernaut Facebook has embraced a similar paradigm. The proliferation of these platforms helped establish a more solid foundation for the esports industry by not only concentrating viewership and building pathways for a distributed fandom to interact, but also by providing a mechanism through which revenue could flow for both large and small operators. Previously, esports monetization had largely been tethered to wins (tournament prize purses) or corporate sponsorship (which outside of some of the notables above, were difficult to come by in these early years). Twitch allowed for easy access to direct community support via subscribers, opportunities to monetize around ads, and in general establish platforms for gaming creators and organizations to both establish and profit from audiences. In short, it was both a better-fit distribution platform as well as a mechanism through which additional money could be pumped into the ecosystem (the final step of this monetization evolution is something we'll address in the final "era" outlined here).

During the early days of Twitch, it helped that one of the most popular games at the time was one that not only continued the legacy of one of the most important games in esports, but was (arguably, one of the first games from a major publisher) designed with professional competition in mind: *Starcraft II*. Basically, every game that becomes a fixture in esports has a competitive mode that pits human opponents against others. It may sound counterintuitive considering the current popularity of esports, but prior to this point very few of them were created with an eye towards being a legitimate competitive platform. However, as is the case with much of gaming history (and in particular, esports history), some of the biggest innovations still came not from the publishers, but from the larger community via modifications on these titles.

It was from community-made modifications that one of the most popular esports genres was born: Massive Online Battle Arenas (MOBAs). The origination of MOBAs from a free mod built upon a popular game to billion-dollar franchises is a confusing web of semi-anonymous programmers, lawsuits, and big-publisher acquisitions. For the sake of brevity, we'll focus on the two most popular end-product franchises: *Defense of the Ancients* (*Dota*) and *League of Legends* (LOL). These titles are notable not only because they are rooted in community modding, but also because they are further demonstrations of the power of free-to-play monetization models in modern gaming, to the point of radically impacting the world of esports. Notably, *Dota* publisher Valve tapped into both the impact of community and the proceeds from the free-to-play model of *Dota* by having portions of *Dota* in-game sales contribute to the prize purse of The International, the championship for the *Dota* esports scene. The result are some of the biggest prize pools in esports today, regularly amounting to tens of millions of dollars since 2014.[6]

What we will refer to as the Networked era is an important interval where esports rose from the ashes of a burst bubble attributable to conforming to the hurdles of traditional media. Somewhat ironically, the birth of Twitch from Justin.tv was also spurred by the fact that showcasing legacy media content via the streaming service was regularly challenged (notably, legal battles with Mixed Martial Arts broadcasts).[7] For the marketing and other sundry business readers, such statements outlining the limitations of legacy platforms and media content might seem heretical. And yet, the reality is that the conventions of media consumption in agency media planning are increasingly far from the realities of how media is consumed, particularly among younger consumers. Even as TV viewership dwindles, overall investment among brands on TV advertising remains relatively stable—this is not to say that esports or esports fans don't need TV, but rather that TV needs entertainment platforms like esports and the legions of fans it commands. We may simply not yet be at the point where a healthy convergence is possible aside from occasional showcases.

And while it should be understood that the gaming content on these platforms isn't exclusively esports (we'll discuss streaming more generally later, to understand the intersection of gaming, esports, and more generalized content produced on these platforms), during this period we also find game studio design decisions to begin to incorporate esports, and grassroots community efforts to have a significant influence upon the entire trajectory of the industry.

If this sounds reminiscent of the tug-of-war between community and business interests we opened this chapter with, it's because that is indeed the case. The final era represents more such push and pulls—publishers reclaiming the trajectory of the competitions around their games, efforts to push the commercialization of esports into a mold that marketers and decision makers could more easily understand, and actors within the industry outside of the game publishers further diversifying the ways they monetize their fan bases.

The New Professionalized Era (aka the Content Era) of Esports (2016–Now)

In 2016, The Overwatch League (OWL) was launched by Blizzard Entertainment as a structured, professional league built around worldwide FPS hit *Overwatch*. Complete with city-based teams, minimum salaries, and healthcare for players, and less explicit focus on prize money, the Overwatch League borrowed heavily from the structure of traditional sports in an effort to create an enduring and stable structure for the *Overwatch* esports scene. This also carried the benefit of being highly translatable to sponsorship buyers in the traditional sports marketing world. It is perhaps no coincidence that this same year, ESPN launched a dedicated esports section and traditional sporting organizations were buying stakes in esports franchises.[8]

OWL was not the last nor the first time esports competitions would be structured and controlled by the game publisher. In fact, CGS (you know, that TV series that crashed the early esports industry) had some of these features. The difference in this case is not only stewardship by the creators of the game itself (for better or worse, thereby catering to the fans in a specific way), but the value it generates for the participating entities. Buying a spot in a league like OWL (often for tens of millions of dollars[9]) opened yet another revenue stream wherein the teams could act as a media property with durable assets not exclusively tied to whether the team wins or loses.[10]

Much like the introduction of Twitch, this represents yet another potential revenue stream from teams, who in some cases are building multiple lines of businesses across different tournaments, leagues, and competitions. By diversifying their portfolios they shelter their business from the collapse of a single game, publisher, or content platform (like a TV show). With both social media and streaming sites encompassing hefty portions of the media diet for young consumers, esports-based entities have increasingly become content-creation engines across the digital landscape. As an example, one need look no further than the prolific gaming organization FaZe Clan, perhaps most familiar to those outside the gaming industry as being the first gaming group to appear on the cover of *Sports Illustrated* magazine.[11] Though rooted in esports competition, Faze is perhaps now best described as a lifestyle marketing brand conveying the intersection of urban styling and gaming prowess, complete with lucrative content sponsorship deals with blue-chip brands such as McDonald's.[12]

Even in this world of gaming-studio-controlled competition, OWL was predated by Riot (publisher of *League of Legends*) who took control of esports competitions in the United States and Europe in 2013. This was initially mostly a cost-center for Riot rather than an independent business unit with expectations for profitability. By consolidating and (presumably) improving the quality and coherency of the tournaments through which *League of Legends* is played, esports are largely used as a marketing tool to drive additional players and deeper engagement with the core game (to then monetize fans through in-game purchases).

Both the utilization of esports as game marketing and reliance on free-to-play monetization are key features to another genre that exploded in recent years. The reason that many of you seeking to understand gaming and esports may have been brought to this book is likely attributable to the battle royale juggernaut *Fortnite*.

In a formula first pioneered by (you guessed it!) a modification-one build for military simulation game *ARMA 2: PlayerUnknown's Battlegrounds* (PUBG), first launched in late 2017. The battle royale style–game features a hundred players dropped onto an island with

Good Luck Having Fun

rapidly contracting borders (such that the players are forced closer and closer together) where they must search for weapons and defeat all their opponents until a single winner emerges. In some ways, *Fortnite* (itself built from a different game mode) perfected this model via whimsical and kid-friendly art direction, humor, and intriguing-level design that didn't have to conform to the photorealistic grittiness of PUBG. In addition to smaller competitive events, *Fortnite* publisher Epic pours tens of millions into the prize purse of larger competitions like the *Fortnite Championship Series*.[13]

These early battle royale giants were also among the first to allow for cross-play across multiple devices, including mobile (i.e., a player can use a single profile, complete with various cosmetics and achievements, to play the core game with others on their PC, game console, or mobile phone). Though most popular on the Asian content at this time and growing in the shadow of the broader esports industry, mobile esports represent a larger trend we'll touch upon more as we think about the future of the gaming ecosystem. PUBG in particular is among the largest games in this rapidly expanding scene.[14]

The modern esports scene is thus one that is both diversifying its core business while trying to find traction among legacy business practices. It represents an era where game publishers have truly taken a position of power within the industry after recognizing the immense revenue and marketing potential of structured game competitions, thereby creating a firm distinction between those who make money through competition vs. the facilitation of competition.

Overtime: Conclusions and Implications

Despite the long history and progress noted above, the industry is still very much a work in progress. For all the fear that modern esports once again sits on a bubble ripe to burst, no doubt fueled by the occasionally misinformed or bad-faith statistics that seem to inflate the size and influence of the industry, I'd say that this is a mischaracterization. This is not from any special faith put into industry statistics (in fact, I'd describe my orientation as being on the more cynical side) so much as the fact that many important cultural social bedrocks are in place. From esports curricula in universities to collegiate and even high-school teams becoming a mainstay in educational institutions, as increasing numbers of consumers grow up with an interest in gaming, avenues to pursue or view serious competition will increase in kind.

A world where competitive entertainment is increasingly not simply hosted online, but is online-native, and untethered by the rules of physics or anything but the bounds of the human imagination paints a compelling picture of where competitive entertainment may soon be trending. We'll consider this more near the end of this book.

From a business standpoint, the concern for a "bubble burst" is overblown for the simple fact that esports is a phenomenon that does not sit within a singular, monolithic, all-or-none bubble. The industry is increasingly populated by a number of sophisticated actors, businesses, and parent corporations with varying mechanisms through which revenue can flow into and out of the industry. As such, similar to video games, esports are not merely a flash-in-the-pan fad, but present a multitude of opportunities to reach the new millennial/Gen Z heads of households in a manner that respects and understands the medium.

Through this chapter we've established a number of defining attributes of esports that deserve consideration as we discuss the merits of integrations into this space:

- Though esports have a surprisingly long history, the core businesses within are still developing and are semi-volatile.
- Games are often social activities, and esports are the expression of a set of these games being played at an extremely high level beyond the potential of most game players.

- Esports have a long history of community involvement, and business people interacting with esports would do well to understand that the community (rightly) feels ownership over this medium.

- The earliest competitive video game tournaments were largely marketing events—as gaming spread via the proliferation of consumer internet, outside parties beyond the game publishers began to seek methods to profit off of competitive gaming.

- The resulting industry is thus one that includes a number of actors looking to profit from or through professional competition, not entirely dissimilar to traditional sports monetization.

- With some notable exceptions, esports exist largely in an online world via PC platforms. We'll address some of these important exceptions in the next chapter.

- Because of the unique and online nature of esports, viewing has largely been consolidated within online streaming platforms such as Twitch.

- Esports are either an independent business unit or marketing tactic for game publishers, which in turn influences the ways outside entities are integrated into the experience.

One of the more famous idioms in esports is "glhf," often sent to competitors at the start of the match. It's an expression of good sportsmanship that is an acronym for "Good luck, have fun." As for the business of esports and any other developing industry, having fun isn't always a given, and more than a little luck is often the key. In the next chapters, we will discuss the more generalized phenomenon of game streaming before finally turning to additional business considerations in the modern esports world.

Chapter 8

Work to Play and Play to Work

Game Streaming and Streamers

The image of a "gamer" as a lone figure, often relegated to the basement or otherwise out of sight of proper society, was never quite correct. Aside from the exhaustive lengths we're going to throughout this book to illustrate a much broader demographic for gaming than most would suspect, sharing gaming experiences with friends or family has always been woven into the practice of playing video games. From arcades to living room couches, watching a game unfold for the pleasure of the viewing experience (even when divorced from a potential competitive element) is a central component to gaming.

In a similar vein to how those more familiar with traditional media should not have been surprised by the rise of esports, given the inherent competitive fields built into gaming, so goes the concept of internet streaming of games. What we are experiencing is a natural media consumption behavior (watching someone game) elevated to the level of media through network effects across the consumer internet. Regardless, internet streaming as a phenomenon has befuddled many in the traditional media world. Whether it be someone playing a video game, talking about a video game, or even giving an opinion on various types of breakfast cereals, the reaction is usually one of incredulous awe and a statement of "someone wants to watch *that?*"

In a word: *Yup.* The simple fact is folks like to play games, but they also like watching games ... particularly when it's convenient to do so. An estimated 9 billion hours of livestreaming video game content was watched in just Q2 of 2021 (excluding China), a number that has over doubled in just two years.[1] An oft-cited maxim at technology companies is that data wins arguments, and this data seems to say that the miscalibration isn't bizarre preferences among a niche group of individuals, so much as a misunderstanding of what can be considered entertaining video content to legions of fans. The broader industry has considered video gaming and branches such as video game streamers as bizarre out of an ongoing and long-held misunderstanding and miscalibration of consumer taste rather than a phenomenon that developed overnight.

As such, like so many parts of the overall discussion around the video game ecosystem, livestreaming is a unique window into broader shifts that are happening in popular culture through the lens of technological innovation. Even as services such as Netflix are disrupting the popular media landscape for more traditional TV viewership behaviors, streaming is redefining expectations around broadcast entertainment into a mold that is inherently more attuned to participator media consumption.[2] The parallels between other participator factors in the video game industry, such as game modding, should not go unnoticed.

The phenomenon of streaming is often conflated with esports, and I recognize there is risk in including an overview of both phenomena in the same section of the book. While both formats entail the same basic behaviors (a platform through which someone watches a video game being played), and the worlds of game streaming and esports are often interwoven as reciprocal business or marketing strategies, the structure and format of the viewing experience are quite unique. This leads to different motivations for the viewing and performance experience, which we'll illustrate below. In addition, a number of competitive gaming scenes (occasionally considered "esports" but often not) have flourished on streaming platforms, along with the phenomenon of "variety/personality" game streamers.

The discussion of streamers also highlights one of the more fundamental tensions in the world of professionalized video game performances (whether within the context of structured competition or not): the uncomfortable tension arising from making a leisure activity work. In the broader timeline of media formats, livestreaming is still in its infancy, yet promises challenges and opportunities in near-equal proportions.

Smash That Subscribe Button: Streamer Types and Motivations

Video game content on streaming platforms comes in many forms, and is one of the most popular streaming categories in terms of hours due in part to some factors we outlined above: video gaming in general is pervasive, and coming across content related to gaming is quite scarce outside of specific portals such as streaming platforms. While we have previously addressed streaming platforms only in light of how they created an effective and well-fit medium for esports, much of the gaming content on streaming platforms such as Twitch or YouTube Gaming is not strictly esports-related.

Streaming services allow for private play to become public entertainment as a networked broadcast.[3] A streamer does not necessarily have to be a direct participant in the esports industry (e.g., a part of a team, professional player) or even *all that good* at video games to be successful; they must merely be entertaining to a large enough group of people to be successful. It's useful to think of video game streamers in two (and occasionally overlapping) groups: those who stream on the basis of skill and those who stream on the basis of personality.

Skill-based streamers are exactly what you might expect—streamers who draw in viewers based upon a special level of skill or acumen within a game (occasionally with deep specialization, though some streamers run across a multitude of titles). This is often the category that esports pros fall into, though it is not to say streamers of this type lack personality that keeps viewers engaged; it's simply not the principal draw. For example, Seth "Scump" Abner is a professional *Call of Duty* player who participates in professional *Call of Duty* esports at a high level, complete with personal endorsement deals.[4] If you're watching Scump, it's almost certainly not by chance—it's because of his notoriety within *Call of Duty* and your likely interest in both learning more about how to play the game and seeing it done at a professional level (one of the key motivations for watching streaming in general, which we'll address momentarily). While it certainly helps that he is a compelling personality who often weaves humor and trash talk throughout broadcasts to keep viewers engaged, the biggest draw for Scump and similar streamers are their level of skill in gaming.

Unlike more traditional sports, the level of access to pros that platforms provide for fans is unique, and adds to the affective value of esports among dedicated fans. Not all the content is likely to be high-level play; much of it comes in the form of practice and experimentation. At times tedious or even error prone (though failure can be entertaining in its own right), this allows for a unique purview among fans into part of what it takes to be the best. For the pros, streaming services and cultivating a fandom via streaming provides a potential exit strategy for those wishing to retire from the competitive scene. Though esports requires a different type of physical prowess from traditional sports, physical ability matters in the form of reaction time, eyesight, and potential repetitive-use injuries around wrists or hands. Like any kind of competition at a high level, there is also an immense mental toll.[5] Historically, one of the few directly-applicable routes to transfer skills among esports pros was professional poker, and the emergence of streaming services allows for professionals to continue to monetize their hard-earned skills in games in a more direct way.

Skill-based streamers also extend to areas of competitive video gaming that are popular yet not generally considered esports in the traditional sense. One of the best examples is the concept of "speedrunning." The act of speedrunning is exceeding simple—individuals compete to complete a game or objective in a game, within a certain set of pre-determined parameters, as quickly as possible. With roots in the early 1990s via fans of titles like *DOOM* and *Quake*, various speedrunning categories and records exist across thousands of games today[6] (inclusive of titles that by design might take upwards of 40–100 hours to complete). The modern speedrunning community at times employs a dizzying (and amusing) array of technical glitches combined with precision execution to clear objectives in astounding times—even heating up game consoles on a hot plate to trigger specific glitches (seriously).[7] The mix of skill, humor, and convention-breaking competition allows for ostensibly any game to be competitive, and serve as a cultural touch point for gaming fans more generally.[8] Organizations like "Games Done Quick" which organize speedrunning marathons, have raised over $31 million since 2010.[9]

Conversely, personality-based streamers are those that draw crowds based primarily on being what is essentially a one-person (typically, though occasionally more) variety show. Often featuring game play prominently, the point isn't necessarily to view individuals who are at the top of their literal and proverbial game, but rather have amassed a following based more on how they connect with audiences. The most famous example is undoubtedly Felix "PewDiePie" Kjellberg, who rose to fame streaming *Minecraft* but has since crafted a streaming empire earning millions of dollars across a variety of different topics.[10] Similar to the discussion of skill-based players, this is not to say that personality-based streamers are not skilled at the games they showcase (though some occasionally bank on their uneven skills in an endearing way), but rather rely on their capability to entertain more generally through the game play performance.

An example of someone on the higher end of the skill bracket who still likely nonetheless fits more in the personality bucket is perhaps the only video game "celebrity" that you, your (potential) children, and grandmother could all recognize by name: Tyler "Ninja" Blevins. Originally a professional *Halo* player, Blevins rose to near-rockstar fame on the crest of *Fortnite* streaming at the height of its popularity, and gained wide notoriety by smashing the audience record (by over 50 percent) on Twitch by streaming with rapper Drake.[11] While Blevins is exceedingly skilled at the games he plays, much of his appeal comes from the family-friendly nature of his stream and charismatic commentary throughout.[12]

Because issues of representation are problematic in competitive gaming, this phenomenon is semi-reflected in the make-up of game streamers. Though female and minority game fans regularly run into similar problems related to harassment, the relative lack of barriers around these platforms has allowed for a more diverse community of personality and skill-based streamers than what is reflected through more "official" esports channels or tournaments. This is not to say that streaming platforms are more of a safe haven for those who don't conform to the "traditional gamer" demographic—in recent months Twitch has been under pressure to clamp down on "hate raids," where streams largely hosted by women or minorities are deluged with slurs.[13] Despite the occasionally inhospitable conditions, streamers such as Maria "ChicaLive" Lopez and Rumay "itsHAFU" Wang have accumulated millions of followers based on their prowess in games ranging from first-person shooters to collectible card games, respectively. The most followed female account on Twitch is among the most followed on the platform in general at well over 8 million followers—Imane "pokimane" Anys (who, as we will discuss in the subsequent chapter, is now in the business of easing barriers around connecting businesses to streaming content creators).

In all cases, it's important to note that the entertainment provided by the streams is typically through the medium of games, but it is the streamers themselves that are the "main act," so to speak. In some cases, this is advantageous—content creators, including but not limited to larger esports or gaming organizations outside of publishers, can be at the whims of game publishers. Games may suddenly have support withdrawn or changed in a fundamental way that impacts the overall dynamics around game play. Streamers can often successfully navigate from game to game, not entirely unlike esports or gaming orgs that have professionals across multiple titles in part to "diversify" their talent bench (to an extent—if a streamer is particularly well known for game play around a specific title, it can be jarring to their community to switch). It is the affinity for a given personality that keeps subscribers or followers engaged, potentially across a wide variety of IP. Though streamers tend to focus on specific genres, like all UGC, there is an inherent variability in content that can and should be expected, either by fans or potential partners.

Between these two broad types of streamers and innumerable types of content produced, a number of potential entertainment needs can be satiated. T. L. Taylor, an MIT scholar who studies a variety of topics in new media ranging from gaming to online streaming, outlines six motivations behind viewership:[14]

1. **Aspirational:** Those looking to become better game players through any number of potential definitions, though often the default motivation for viewers new to streaming.
2. **Educational:** Aspirational usually matures to educational. If you want to be the best, you'll want to learn from the

best—watching esports pros or other highly skilled streamers provides tangible benefits to the game play of individuals in addition to their own potential streaming performances.

3. **Inspirational:** Those that are deep into a given game fandom (be it a specific title, genre, or otherwise) will seek to watch others who share their level of fandom. As noted, the outlets for gaming content to be consumed are often relatively limited, so game streamers occupy a large overall share of potential content within some fandoms.

4. **Entertainment:** Generally the principal draw to any stream is the pleasure of watching it. Though skill and personality-based streamers may have different styles through which they will entertain an audience, in either case they are producing content that is entertaining by tapping one of the other potential motivations.

5. **Community:** Initially the biggest innovation of Twitch relative to incumbent rival YouTube, streaming services incorporate increasingly sophisticated functionality for viewers to communicate with the host of the stream and one another. In-jokes, memes, and other cultural artifacts can be regularly viewed within the chats of popular streamers.

6. **Ambiance:** Have you ever flipped on the TV to have some "noise" in the background, even if you aren't really viewing the show? Same deal—for many individuals (particularly younger generations), streaming services act in the same media use-case as linear TV (often as a whole-cloth replacement). As such, sometimes folks just want something on "in the background" even if they are not directly engaged.

An ongoing refrain throughout this book is to understand the motivations not just of the end-user, but the producer of gaming content. Similar to streaming viewers, streaming creators have a multitude of different reasons and motivations for sharing their forays into gaming in a public space. Taylor[15] similarly identifies key motivations (aside from potential revenue) for individuals who stream:

- **Social connections:** Streaming is a two-way street as it pertains to community. As much as viewers are looking for camaraderie from the streaming personality and other viewers, the inverse is true for the content-creator. One may go so far as to even note that strong connectivity with their fandom is a prerequisite for a successful streamer.

- **Transforming the play experience:** Some folks like to have an audience, and some activities are well suited to one. Even among more causal streamers, some of the initial needs that streaming satisfies is a deeper play experience through potentially sharing it with like-minded others.

- **Creativity and performance:** The livestream is a versatile pallet for any number of creative endeavors, including things like "stage presence" or even the craft of on-screen graphics. Streamers often operate as single-person businesses of sorts (even those that don't monetize in a serious way), making the experience and act of stage-craft for their stream its own reward.

- **Professional aspirations:** Many streamers start through influence from other streamers with the aspiration of cultivating and growing fandoms of their own, complete with potential financial rewards.

- **Professional expectations:** As noted throughout, streaming services serve a key role in the world of esports not simply for the purposes of official tournament broadcast, but as promotional and content creation mechanisms for professional esports organizations. Many esports pros have minimum streaming hours built into their contract as part of their official duties for the organization, ostensibly to construct a robust content series.

Streamers and streaming services thus fulfill a multitude of needs within the overall media ecosystem of increasingly networked generations of consumers, with gaming being a central form of content in this ecosystem. Like all the forms of gaming discussed throughout this book, streaming is a highly affective medium through the occasionally deep personal connections that can form between a streamer and the audience. This level of affect raises potential risks for both the audience and streamer.

The most notable risk among any user-generated content, but in particular content that is created and largely hinges on the personality of a given person, is that it is created by and promotes a person … and people occasionally do things that are questionable. The world of professional streamers, even those at the apex of the craft, have been subject to any number of controversies. "PewDiePie" Kjellberg, noted above as an exemplar of personality-based streamers, is unfortunately also an exemplar of problematic streaming personalities. Kjellberg has been routinely accused of anti-Semitic behaviors and symbols, notably via a bombshell investigation by the *Wall Street Journal*.[16] Streaming mega-star Hershel "Dr. DisRespect" Beaham IV took his always-on persona a bit too far by livestreaming in the bathroom of landmark video game industry event E3,[17] among a more recent and (at the time of publication) permanent ban from Twitch for reasons unknown. Streamers are human, and humans make mistakes or otherwise exhibit behaviors we don't endorse—this presents a risk to both fans and businesses when there are rifts between the values of the streaming personality and the individual or brand.

For the streamers, though often far from the streets of Hollywood, it is possible to attain a certain level of fame—when viewers and followers on various streaming platforms or social media reach the millions, this is an inevitability. Like any type of celebrity, this comes at a cost—stories of unhealthy fixation on streamers from fans are common, in addition to a threat that is somewhat unique to streaming and sadly present from nearly the onset of the development of streaming platforms: "swatting." Justin.tv, the progenitor of Twitch, was tested by founder Justin Kan by essentially livestreaming the entirety of his life. This ranged from the mundane (eating lunch) to the highly questionable (going on a date). Viewers soon found that they could "prank" Kan by reporting a police emergency, a phenomenon later dubbed as swatting, and led to the San Francisco police bursting into his apartment and demanding an explanation from Kan (hands in the air)—all live and for the world to see.[18] The risk of swatting has become an unfortunately and potentially deadly reality for streamers, where often the most popular streamers have had to reach out to local police departments to establish a working relationship in order to prevent the police from responding to bad-faith calls for help.

On a more practical basis, the "business" of streaming is one where content creators are the producer, set-creator, accountant, scheduler, and talent all wrapped into one. This does, of course, speak to one of the key advantages to streaming services—there are low barriers of entry to get started, often only requiring minimal set-up with regard to specialized software like OBS Studio. However, stream set-ups can become as involved as incorporating sophisticated cameras and microphones, dedicated computers to run streaming and/or chat software, multiple monitors to assess the product, specialized lighting and props, and so on. While one of the key motivations for streamers often includes the technical and artistic challenges of producing this content, it also represents a potential area of strain, particularly when coupled with real or imagined pressures to keep up with a set "schedule" for streaming.

The net result is that even if a given streamer starts a journey from a more basic desire to enhance their play experience, there remains a fundamental tension between when "play" becomes "work," as motivations and needs between the "play" state of mind increasingly conflate with the "work" state of mind. Streamers, like esports professionals, have play "contaminated" by reality, obligation, and professionalism, thereby almost certainly altering their relationship to gaming and (potentially) the root cause of bad behaviors or burnout.[19]

Watch This Space: Conclusions and Implications

As we'll discuss in subsequent chapters around implications for brand integrations, there are a multitude of potential opportunities within streaming platforms beyond "traditional" ad buys, including working directly with streaming personalities in a framework similar to digital influencer marketing. Various platforms have differing mechanisms through which a streamer can interact with their audience and vice versa (via commercial means and otherwise), though the broad pattern for outside parties is that the streamers themselves can carry massive brands that resonate with wide swathes of the gaming fandom.

The type of entertainment these personalities provide ranges from displays of skill to de facto variety shows (or somewhere in between) via the medium of game play, which triggers a number of potential motivations for fans, often with deep affective connections. Understanding the relative motivations of the streaming personalities themselves also allows for a more productive and beneficial dialogue between potential partners—as we've continued to see, exchanges of value, understanding, and displays of authenticity are the bedrock for effective integrations. With all highly affective marketing channels, a deeper level of understanding allows for potential missteps that could amount to a lack of authenticity at best, and to exploitation at worst.

While streaming services offer a number of categories and content types beyond gaming, ranging from the absurd (Jack Dire regularly streams ... a jar of peanut butter) to the provocative (such as the controversial world of hot tub streaming[20]), the foundation of gaming content provides a multitude of benefits within the gaming ecosystem—revenue streams for gaming content creators (inclusive of esports organizations), communities for fandoms across any number of games, effective and creative marketing opportunities for games, and so on. Though any type of personality-driven marketing (be it influencer, streaming, or the combination of the two) carries potential risks, the payoff is a flexible and creative palette to reach often-elusive audiences *en masse*.

Chapter 9

Unbalanced

Opportunities in Game Viewing for Businesses

A s was the case with opportunities in gaming, the leadup to discussing more general opportunities for integration in esports or streaming was prefaced with considerable background on the wider industry of viewing gaming content. The rationale for this approach is similar to that of gaming itself, although with some key differences. In the case of integrating with consumers who are either playing or viewing a game, a deeper understanding of a not well-known ecosystem is of paramount importance for successful integrations—potentially more so in in the world of game viewing, which leans more towards "traditional" gaming sensibilities with a high valuation on authenticity. Both formats have additionally found it necessary to confront the complex relationship between the growth of the fandom and the economic realities of their businesses, with game viewing at a much earlier stage of maturation.

The case of esports diverges from gaming in that commercialization has always been a more open conversation within the industry since our cultural understanding of anything related to competitive entertainment has a wide palette of acceptability for featuring brand logos or other exogenous messaging. The "how" of this revenue acquisition has, however, become perhaps the most heated debate within the industry more generally, drawing battle lines between early esports proponents intent on keeping the grassroots and passion-based feel of the industry intact versus waves of newcomers to the industry looking to monetize game-viewing content more effectively. Similarly, game streaming has fundamentally relied on fan support even in the early days, with calls for donations and subscriber functionalities partially gamified into the content of the stream or the design of the streaming service.

The potential for integration opportunities for marketers or business decision makers within broader game viewing has the appearance of being "easier" than that of game playing, given the template set by other forms of competitive entertainment (in the case of esports) or broader influencer marketing (in the case of streaming). However, these parallels to other more well-known forms of competitive entertainment (whether traditional sports or otherwise) or influencer marketing has always been a double-edged blade. On the one hand it's a natural jumping-off point for conversations given parallels in practices (including revenue generation). On the other, viewing gaming content has necessarily diverged from more traditional forms of video consumption, due to both the unique nature of this content and larger generational patterns in media consumption.

Specifically, game viewing in the form of esports and streaming is rising on the crest of younger audiences (the coveted 18–34 demographic) preferring streaming services relative to linear TV (cable or broadcast television). Esports came to relative prominence as a buzzy darling of the marketing world because it was an alternative to legacy video programming (including legacy sports), which is largely tethered to linear television, a format that has been on the decline for years (including highly anticipated sporting events such as the Olympics)[1] and yet still commands the lion's share of advertising dollars. As we learned from the history of esports, some of the most visible early faults of the industry were related to fitting the content to the format of TV, thereby obviating much of what made these competitions compelling for its emerging fan base. This is not to say that TV is completely out of the question—gaming content is in some ways remerging on more traditional media channels as the fandom (and therefore, presumed eyeballs) continues to grow, such as the relaunch of gamer-centric G4 TV.[2] However, this relaunch comes with heavy presence on streaming channels—platforms that have become the de facto home of esports and gaming content more generally, in addition to bringing forth a new brand of viewing experiences and talent in the form of streamers.

In summary, engagement with game viewing in the form of streamers or esports is in large part due to the fact that they are digital-native and digital-friendly options for consumers who increasingly watch video content online. Moreover, these same digital-native consumers are broadly eschewing traditional formats such as TV by exhibiting "cord cutting" or "cord nevering" behaviors—they are unlikely to watch broadcast television nor subscribe to traditional cable, in favor of over-the-top (OTT) video streaming services, relative to older consumers.[3] The proliferation of cord-cutting behaviors has created a significant barrier for "casual" TV sports viewing, a long-standing mechanism for drawing in new fans to the traditional sports ecosystem (and one which has often been referenced as a barrier for esports more generally).[4] Decreasing traditional TV viewership combined with diminished opportunities for participation and live viewing of traditional sports (including the considerable costs in doing so)[5] has created fertile ground for esports to shine as a viable alternative. As an example, esports fans (who are overwhelmingly a young, valuable advertising demographic) report fandom levels towards gaming/esports organizations such as FaZe Clan or 100 Thieves as higher or on par with traditional sports teams, including similar levels of followership between sports and gaming influences, according to research by YouGov.[6]

The opportunity presented by game viewing is thus reasonably clear—an ecosystem of video content that is new and emerging yet feels alluringly familiar, while presenting one of the few ways to connect with the ever-elusive younger cohorts of consumers. The similarities between delivery channels (streaming), relative content (gaming), and interested demographic (18–34) has caused much of the broader conflation between "esports" and "streaming." Here again, at the risk of further muddying the waters, we'll consider points of integration in the broader category of "watching game play," given similarities driven by streaming platforms, though with differential areas of focus pending the opportunity:

- **Streaming and Esports Advertising:** Like games, esports and streamers have amassed an audience that is scaled and comprised of a valuable enough demographic to be of keen interest to advertisers, and traditional advertising across these experiences is similarly one of the most accessible methods of integration. Given the relative flexibility and ubiquity of advertising within either form of video content, we'll address opportunities across both esports and streaming.

- **Esports Sponsorships:** The concept of sponsorship aligned with competitive entertainment can be traced back thousands of years,[7] and may very well continue this legacy well into the digital era. Sponsorships are the foundational revenue source for the esports ecosystem, and in many ways they provide some of the most flexible opportunities for outside entities.

- **Streaming Influencer and Content Marketing:** Savvy gaming organizations have shifted focus from not simply notching impressive wins, but formulating more holistic lifestyle brands for their fandoms. The result is that individual streams and larger gaming groups have become skilled at creating compelling content. The emphasis here will be on streamers as gaming influencers more generally, though important implications for esports will be addressed throughout.

As was the case with opportunities in gaming more generally, we'll address these opportunities roughly in order from least to most resource-intensive points of integration. In another parallel to our discussion of gaming opportunities, our goal is not to outline every tactical consideration or point of entry. From a pragmatic view, this would be a tedious and low-value endeavor—where examples and guides exist for these integrations, they are exhaustive (namely, for advertising in streaming services). Where they do not exist, as is the case of sponsorships or leveraging influencers, the execution of tactics is so customized that a step-by-step guide would be folly.

As such, our goal is once again to formulate a strategic framework to address the broader opportunities across game viewing, which can in turn be applied to any given tactical deployment, with appropriate grounding in the larger historical, psychological, and logistical considerations addressed in the preceding chapters. We can summarize some of these key considerations as:

- Balancing the legitimization brought by alignment with mainstream brands or entities against the need to remain authentic to more "traditional" gaming audiences.

- Growing an emerging audience while partially limiting distribution to specific channels (largely various streaming outlets).

- Navigating a complex web of stakeholders with unequal power over the games serving as the basis of game viewing content.

- Intense fragmentation across the landscape, wherein fandom can be split among any combination of games, teams, tournaments, or even individual talent.

- A wider industry reckoning with declining audiences in traditional sports[8] against a need to find younger audiences who were previously engaged with traditional sports programming.

- Managing the tension of "play as work" and producing streaming content against the rising prominence of gaming influencers with younger consumers.

With these considerations in mind, it bears mentioning that the title of this chapter is deliberate—when something is "unbalanced" in a game, it means that there is an unfair advantage given to a side or aspect of a game environment. Such imbalances have the potential to create an unfair advantage built into the fundamental design of the game. Often multiple iterations of "patches" or other modifications by developers are released to account for imbalances, though "balancing" a game is something that is never truly finished, given that players (particularly from a more competitive vantage point) have become exceedingly talented at capitalizing on any potential advantage (intended by the developers or not) afforded by the game. One can view the broader game viewing ecosystem, and the opportunities for integration therein, in a similar light—it's a system with innumerable unequal advantages, competing sides, and stakes that are still in need of cycles of iteration to make a more balanced and equitable industry for those facilitating competitive gaming.

This is not meant to dissuade interested parties; it merely serves to underline the point that, at this time, opportunities in game viewing can largely be described as "emerging." Though aspects of these opportunities such as esports (or even the simple pleasures of watching someone game) have histories as long as gaming itself, the modern world of consuming game content has only become more manifest in the past decade or so (roughly earmarked with the rise of platforms such as Twitch). With any newer form of emerging media there is a learning curve, and both the broader game viewing industries in addition to marketers and businesses executives seeking to tap this audience are still in early stages. As has been the case throughout this book, a little understanding and orientation towards the industry can go a long way towards success that entails more than a "first(ish) mover" advantage, but broader experience in not just orientating strategies towards emergent platforms such as streaming, but toward fandoms and competitions.

Play Breaks: Esports and Streaming Advertising

For all the newness underlying these forms of content creation, the fundamental currency of media remains attention, and that attention is monetized via ads. Like direct gaming opportunities, digital advertising directly within, or adjacent to, gaming content broadcasts are both the most turnkey and scalable formats for entry. Game streaming has become an attractive target for ad buys, given the relative difficulty of finding younger audiences across the increasingly fragmented digital media landscape. Streaming content has the advantage of being able to command attention for more than a few seconds (relative to, say, flicking through a feed-based social media app) due in large part to the draw of the talent creating the content, coupled with the convenience/familiarity of purchasing inventory in digital mainstays such as YouTube.

As a result, purchasing advertisements directly through these streaming sites may be as simple as an adjustment in targeting across campaigns already planned for by a marketer or business with a desire to integrate into gaming content. The relative ubiquity of YouTube (and increasingly, platforms such as Twitch) means there is no shortage of exacting comparisons of placements (ranging from pre- to mid-content via pre-roll and mid-roll video ads, respectively);

for our purposes one distinction is semi-unique to esports or generalized game streaming and therefore calls for due discussion: the differentiation between "native" and "stitched" placements.

"Native" placements are those that, intuitively enough, are native to streaming platforms and can be purchased directly from them. The ability to offer these placements is often the direct commercial upside from streaming platforms in securing exclusivity with gaming entities ranging from leagues to individual streamers. However, the younger skew of this audience is as much a liability as an asset in digital media buying: While estimates of utilization of digital ad blockers varies as wide as 25–50 percent of the digital population,[9] there is near-universal agreement that uptake of these technologies is much more common with younger audiences. In other words, the very audience that makes opportunities in gaming and esports viewing valuable, insofar that they may be disproportionately reached via ads with this content, is also disproportionately invested in avoiding ads at all costs. Services such as Twitch, where much of the content is gaming-oriented, has had to grapple with this reality by efforts ranging from differential placements meant to defeat ad-blocking software[10] to direct appeals to reason.[11]

The most effective way to "defeat" an ad blocker is to make it really, really difficult to determine how or where an ad is being served. This is the basic premise of "stitched" placements, which are those that include a given advertisement placed directly within the streamed content by the content provider (as opposed to inserted by the streaming provider). Such placements, which in some cases are brokered as part of larger sponsorship deals, have the advantage of being "unblockable" but are much more narrow in scope. Whereas an ad placement directly with a streaming service can be conveniently (and nearly instantaneously) purchased via a dizzying array of advertising technologies and scaled across any number of different types of content on the platform, stitched ads must be inserted well in advance of the broadcast content (whether it's an esports match or more generalized stream) and offers significantly less flexibility because it is confined to the particular publisher or content creator through which the deal was brokered. However, as was the case in game advertising, working directly with a content producer allows for advertising "breaks" to be inserted more naturally in the content, whereas pre-roll inventory might suffer from longer view-times relative to other content on streaming platforms and mid-roll inventory might create an obtrusive experience.

In summary, the convenience and flexibility of native placements come with a liability related to generalized obtrusiveness and blocking efforts, whereas stitched placements occupy a space somewhere between the more turnkey native placements and larger sponsorship activations. The "right" choice between the two is thus entirely dependent on the needs of the advertiser, though generally a more well-fit placement will enjoy better acceptability from the sensibilities of the esports and gaming audience (as partially demonstrated by the high uptake of ad blockers among this audience), something that native placements afford better access to in addition to being a lighter-weight articulation of broader sponsorship activations.

Play of the Game: Esports Sponsorships

The historical value of sponsorships in competitive entertainment, put simply, has been to have the affinity a fan has for a given sport, team, or star reflected upon the sponsoring entity. This remains true in the world of esports, within additional and unique value generated by the fact that it is an emerging ecosystem: lending legitimacy. Fans of esports and generalized gaming content are invested in the viability and future of a landscape to which (not unlike gaming more generally) they feel immense connection to the point of ownership. Marks from an entity in dominant culture dwelling in this ecosystem draw connections between a competitive scene on the outskirts of popular culture toward the center. This desire for legitimization, passion among the fandom, and relatively uncluttered space for outside branding to be present (the average number of sponsors in an esports broadcast is far less than, say, NASCAR or the NFL) yields a sponsorship experience that can potentially capture attention above and beyond more general streaming content or even traditional sports, as demonstrated by comparative studies.[12]

Sponsorships are a unique focus for esports insofar as they represent the majority of revenue in the ecosystem. Recent reports have estimated that 60 percent of the revenue in global esports is generated from sponsorships, and only 20 percent from media rights with platforms like Twitch or YouTube.[13] Locking up esports content to specific platforms, while favorable from a revenue perspective, does insert hurdles for growth when the content isn't quite as ubiquitous as it could be online,[14] and isn't nearly as lucrative as traditional sports where an entity like the NHL earned $625 million per year despite having about the same viewership as a single esports league.[15] The relatively heftier focus on sponsorships within esports is thus partially a reflection of disproportionate valuations placed on linear viewership and the uncomfortable fit of broadcast exclusivity in a digital world, though multiyear agreements have subsidized part of the operating costs of hosting leagues and tournaments similar to traditional sports while securing significant sources of content for the streaming platforms.[16]

As much as sponsorships hold greater importance in the world of esports relative to other forms of competitive entertainment, the "where" and "how" of sponsorship in esports is complicated by the unique array stakeholders present in the esports ecosystem. The biggest differentiation from more traditional sports is the simple fact that no one "owns" the game of (say) baseball or basketball, but someone very much owns the games of *League of Legends* or *Counter-Strike*. Moreover, the very rules of these games can be changed at a whim according to these publishers, or shut down entirely. This stokes a fundamental tension between game publishers and esports organizations, including an inherent need for diversification among these organizations across several games or tournaments both as a means to maximize audiences and to de-risk reliance on any given game or game publisher.

Similar to the diversification of audiences in esports, so too are the entities through which sponsorships are possible, given differential areas of dominion in esports. Each of these stakeholders has varying levels of influence over the broader ecosystem, and often affords unique opportunities for integration pending their vantage point within the industry.

Publishers and Games (Examples: *Epic*, Valve, Activision Blizzard)

At risk of stating the glaringly obvious, there are no esports without the electronic games. Game publishers have had occasionally waning interest and influence in the development of esports. Early proponents later became somewhat hostile to the idea (Nintendo), some have specifically designed games with the understanding that they would be viable competitive platforms (Activision Blizzard and *Starcraft 2*, Riot and *Valorant,* etc.), whereas some of the biggest games in esports owe more to community modifications than the developers of the core games themselves (e.g., *League of Legends* and *Dota*, both as antecedents to Activision Blizzard's *Warcraft 3*).

Game developers and publishers arguably have the greatest influence over the texture of the esports industry, and their ongoing approach to wielding it is as diverse as the historical precedents.

Some choose to be somewhat hands off with the competitive scene (such as Valve, publisher of *Counter-Strike* and *Dota*) and/or largely use it as a marketing mechanism for in-app purchases or the core game,[17] whereas others control the full funnel from the game itself to associated leagues and team structures (such as Riot with *League of Legends* Esports or Activision Blizzard with the *Overwatch* and *Call of Duty* leagues), often with distinct corporate entities.

As one might suspect, the "full funnel" publishers have the widest array of opportunities to offer, ranging from more stand-ard sponsorship activations to the potential for in-game integra-tions (à la those prevalent in gaming more generally). This does not, however, imply a completely open creative canvas for esports supported by these publishers—the operative word in the description above is that the esports and partnerships organizations within game publishers are often *independent*. In other words, not entirely unlike more baseline game integrations, the partnership's organizations must work with the developers, where a healthy tension always exists between the creative endeavor of game development and commercialization via outside integrations. In more extreme cases, the occasionally fledgling nature of the competitive scene around a game can be viewed as a distraction rather than an asset by developers, creating a tug-of-war between development and broader business interests.

Leagues and Tournaments

Many opportunities around specific titles or game franchises are thus wholly consolidated by the game publishers; however, independ-ent leagues and tournament structures not directly under control of the game publishers have existed for basically as long as esports. As an example, the Electronic Sports League (ESL) has been opera-tional since 2000 and hosts a variety of international tournaments in partnership with publishers that run their own leagues directly aligned with their game franchises (such as *Blizzard* and *Riot*) in addition to games that don't have a publisher-controlled tournament structure, including blockbuster titles such as *Halo* or fighting game pioneer *Mortal Kombat*.

What these league and tournament structures outside of publisher control lack in the potential depth of the opportunities of full-funnel developers noted above, they make up for in breadth—a larger array of competitive games serves as a partial solve to an already fragmented fan base.

Streaming and Media Platforms

Platforms such as Twitch and YouTube Gaming have become the de facto destinations for all things esports, and occasionally they host tournaments or other esports features aligned with game publishers or larger tournament series (typically as extensions of broader media rights conversations with a given publisher, league, or other competitive industry).

The resulting canvas for integrations is quite broad, including many of the same relative ideas or placements (branded screen wipes, "picture in picture," screen wrappers, etc.) that one might see during a traditional sports match within esports. This is partially due to the influx of commercial talent from traditional sports to esports, ranging from broadcast teams implementing the placements, marketers designing them, and ultimately production crews that have ported over viewership elements that lend to branding opportunities ("play of the game" highlights, match breaks, etc.). For example, food delivery service Grubhub recently closed a three-year partnership with the League Championship Series (LCS, a competitive series for *League of Legends*), which thematically banks on both the delivery and consumption of food, including a sponsored segment called "Delivering the Win" and hosing "Feeding Frenzy" festivities at the LCS championship (including a planned buffalo wings eating contest).[18]

Ultimately, what is possible or permissible within a given league, tournament, or otherwise is largely a negotiation between the organizing entity and potential partners, and valuation of any given portion of the sponsorship often is determined through inexact or antiquated means (including impression counting etc.). This too owes much to the influence of traditional sports in esports—despite the digital legacy of esports and the higher bar for analytics this entails, measurement and effectiveness research has not been a focus area of traditional sports sponsorships. As such, the terms of these negotiations often concentrate on more basic measures such as presumed "reach" of any given broadcast, which gives no credit to the potential branding power or "depth" of affinity that may be reached in any given sponsorship spot. For a final parallel with traditional sports, any given sponsorship is typically positioned as "exclusive" for a given category, meaning that that potential "fits" for integrations must be mutually agreed upon by both the partner and the hosting entity.

Determining the best area of entry for esports sponsorships is therefore a rough heuristic that includes availability and relevance of partner fit (inclusive of brand safety—some outside partners might not wish to be aligned with FPS competitions, as a typical example), scale of the tournament in question (many esports are inherently global, which may or may not be relevant to the partner), and fitting the attributes of the partner brand or marks with the competition in a way that reflects mutual balance and fit. The depth and scope of these partnerships is likely to vary considerably between "full funnel" esports developers (likely very deep but somewhat narrow in scope) vs. independent tournaments/leagues and streaming platforms (less deep due to lack of IP ownership, but potentially much broader).

Streaming Influencer and Content Marketing

The array of leagues, games, tournaments, or broader organizations that afford sponsorship opportunities are numerous, yet the unifying trait across these choices is that gaming serves as not just the competitive space, but also the broader cultural backdrop for a deeply invested fandom. More simply, the association that is being sold is for an outside entity to be integrated into the more "traditional" aspects of the gaming lifestyle in an authentic way—a strategic means of ingress that is perhaps best epitomized by influencer and content marketing by individual streamers or gaming organizations.

The digital-native nature of esports and streaming has, not entirely like the broader contours of the industry, created a special kind of celebrity for content creators in gaming, in part by allowing for unparalleled access not just to gaming content, but also to the players and personalities behind the content. Whether it be by skill within a given game, an entertaining way of presenting the game, or some combination of both, streamers and gaming organizations have mastered the art of making compelling viewing experiences out of game play or exploring broader aspects of the gaming fandom. The business of game viewing, whether competitive/skill-based or more personality driven, is now foundationally based upon influencer marketing and content creation, in a departure from traditional revenue sources such as ticket sales or consumer products (though still present) or early-days reliance on prize purses.

Gaming influencers are quickly becoming one of the largest categories in the broader influencer marketing landscape, particularly among men 18–24, where it is the most followed group of influencers globally.[19] As a result, individual streamers can command audiences in the millions—leaked data from Twitch demonstrated that some streamers receive payouts in the millions of dollars between advertising and subscriber revenue drawn from their expansive fan bases.

However, the number of streamers who reach this level of exposure is vanishingly small—25 percent of the top 10,000 earning streamers make less than minimum wage, and still represent the upper echelon of the some 9 million streamers on Twitch.[20] And while streaming influencers are significantly more diverse in terms of racial, ethnic, or gender identity than what can be found in competitive esports, it is only marginally so—only about 5 percent of young women follow gaming influencers, and the top earning streams on Twitch were overwhelmingly white and male.[21] Working with larger gaming organizations as opposed to individual streamers partially offers a greater range in diversity, as demonstrated by collaborations between Gucci and gaming group 100 Thieves,[22] where popular female streamer Rachell "Valkyrae" Hofstetter (the "Queen of YouTube" and most viewed female streamer on the platform[23]) is a co-owner and is featured prominently in the promotional materials. Similarly, a partnership between McDonald's and the gaming organization FaZe Clan called "Spotlight" was specifically designed to elevate diverse voices in gaming, including Black members of FaZe Clan speaking to their experiences as Black gamers.[24]

As such, while the broader enterprise of game viewing continues to struggle with representation, streaming provides potential routes for more inclusive strategies. Utilization of gaming influencers for generalized influencer marketing or content creation thus requires due consideration of the audience to be reached as much as the context through which they will be reached. This is partially a consequence of demographic skews in both representation and audience, but also the platform through which the influencer(s) work—as much as media rights are a reality for esports, exclusive contracts for top streamers on platforms like YouTube, Twitch, or Facebook Gaming are becoming commonplace, arguably kicked off in late 2019 when

Tyler "Ninja" Blevins signed a multimillion-dollar deal with now-defunct streaming platform Mixer.[25]

The drum beat of multimillion-dollar deals has led some groups to eye lofty valuations amounting to the billions for some gaming groups.[26] Whether it is one of these gaming organizations or an individual with an expansive fan base, the business of game influencers seeks the same general value: leveraging the authentic voice and talent of those deeply immersed in the larger culture of gaming to present a message in a cogent manner. The most successful streamers and gaming organizations are those that have threaded the needle towards not just making content that is compelling for gaming audiences, but content that can be broadly profitable for partnerships, inclusive of leveraging their fan base across the broader media ecosystem. Top gaming influencers such as Olajide Olayinka Williams "JJ" Olatunji, who goes by the handle KSI, can have millions of followers on platforms such as Instagram valuing any given post on such sites at upwards of $200,000 based on the value of the impressions generated.[27]

To build audiences of this scale, influencers and content creators have developed a well-trained sense for what will, or will not, resonate with their audiences. As a result, not entirely unlike esports sponsorships, leveraging these talents as a means for integration with the broader gaming ecosystem is not so much a choice given to the partner as much as a mutually agreeable arrangement between the partner and influencer. While identifying a given influencer that speaks to a specific viewer motivation that is aligned with the goals of a given strategy (e.g., education, inspirational, more generalized entertainment) can be a productive first step, a given message or brand that will not resonate with the influencer's audience is unlikely to be worthwhile to the influencer at the cost of authenticity. Similarly, due diligence on the behalf of the partner on the common behaviors and practices of the individual or organization can avoid the misalignments in messaging (as noted in the preceding chapter on streaming, even the most popular streamers may have foibles in the past that should be considered).

The prospects of the partnership can be quite broad—but ultimately some degree of creative control will inevitably be in the hands of the influencer or content creator. Being specific on the value proposition to their audience (including incentives, if applicable), and desired outcomes can aid initial alignment,[28] but finding the right partnership may inevitably be a labor-intensive process involving vetting talent and aligning on the right personality fit. In partial reaction to this friction, an emerging trend in the broader ecosystem to create more common ground between interested partners and content creators is the founding of specialized agencies or talent groups, such as RTS (notably founded by one of the few aforementioned female mega-star streamers, Imane "Pokimane" Anys).[29] As viewership around gaming content becomes more normalized and ubiquitous, so too will the similar supporting structures. Whether leveraging such an agency or otherwise, understanding the unique pressures of game streaming, in addition to the craft and dedication required to produce compelling content that resonates with a discerning audience will create a platform for earnest conversations.

Thanks for Stopping By: Conclusions and Implications

The growing influence of gaming is nowhere more apparent than in the diversity of entertainment content structured around it, be it competitive or otherwise. Internet streaming services have provided a platform where formerly niche or localized activities, such as watching game play, have been scaled to the masses. In doing so, flexible means of monetization for developing industries such as esports in addition to natural points of integration for interested partners have been brought forth. The opportunity to legitimize a fan's favored competitive sport, or support their favorite gaming personality, offers a uniquely digital-native means to reach some of the most elusive audiences in the broader media landscape.

Though nearly all opportunities for integrating with game viewing behaviors are manifest through streaming services, the strategies for doing so have a number of potential tradeoffs and advantages. Not unlike opportunities in gaming, we can summarize these across a number of (slightly different) axes ranging from monetary/time investment to the relative level of authenticity offered by the opportunity (see Table 9.1).

Similar to integrations with gaming, the easiest and broadest places to start are via advertisements, where any number of potential agencies or organizations can offer immense experience in serving media on platforms like YouTube or Twitch. Messaging that will potentially resonate in game environments requires more nuance, and is another area where working directly with a game developer that has a partnerships arm that covers esports can provide a fast track. However, independent agencies that work with a variety of league structures or content creators, or traditional agencies that are building dedicated gaming expertise, will increasingly be able to provide direction on what tactics to connect towards a broader strategy.

Regardless of the point of ingress, the parallels to more traditional forms of entertainment must be contextualized against the unique need state, circumstances, and technologies that have become common for viewing behaviors around gaming content. Game viewing represents not just the influence of gaming on the media consumption of younger consumers, but also fundamental shifts in expectations

Table 9.1 A Summary of Opportunities in Esports

	Streaming Advertisements	Esports Sponsorships	Streaming Influencer and Content Marketing
Monetary investment	*Low*	*Moderate to high*	*Moderate to high*
Time investment	*Low*	*Moderate to high*	*High*, particular in relation to finding and formalizing an agreement
Authenticity	*Low to moderate*, with "stitched" advertisements more likely to naturally fit within the streaming content	*Moderate to high*, pending fit and how the activation is brought to life adjacent to the competition	*High*, assuming that the upfront diligence has been done between potential interest from the creator's fan base and the message at stake
Resonance	*Low to moderate*, here too, pending how well the ad can be integrated in the stream (and related, the extent to which it may be blocked)	*Moderate to high*, here too pending how well the message can be integrated within the broadcast	*High*, influencers and content creators trade on the authenticity, and their recommendation tends to carry immense weight with their audiences

and trends around media more generally. While industries such as esports and complementary content like game streaming are newer entrants to the broader media ecosystem, the opportunities provided go beyond a mere complement to a larger gaming strategy, so much as one that taps into the future of media consumption.

Part III

Storytelling in Virtual Worlds: Future Directions and Conclusions

Life in the Screen

Metaverse and Future Directions

P opular culture has depicted a fairly uniform picture of the future of technology, particularly as it pertains to gaming. We imagine (often dystopian) societies where fully interactive and immersive virtual worlds have in some cases not only become the norm, but a necessary retreat from the everyday. Works such as Neal Stephenson's *Snow Crash* or Ernest Klein's *Ready Player One* paint the picture of a world where the better part of human interactivity exists not just online, but in virtual worlds of our own creation. The similarity of these visions are a reflection of the fact that the human mind tends to drift towards the possibilities of quite literally being within games—either as a fantasy or nightmare (depending on your POV) made manifest.

When we think about future directions for the gaming industry, and how businesses and brands may play into that future, it is not only impossible to address this future without mentioning the budding concept of the metaverse, but it is also helpful to frame the discussion in a way such that we think about the future of all game-adjacent technologies through this same lens. As of the time of writing this book, the conversation around the concept of the metaverse has become a near-deafening one catalyzed in part by Facebook renaming to "Meta" as a serious signal of intent towards building this future vision.[1] As both a company that has deeply shaped the modern internet and how humans communicate through it which also has a history of placing "all-in" directives on technological pathways such as mobile,[2] the entire world took notice.

But what is the metaverse? It is an idea—one that relates to a future vision of the internet that is "embodied," with less demarcation between our physical selves and our digital representations, not entirely unlike the virtual worlds threaded through popular fiction. This entails persistent, virtual worlds (often envisioned as 3D) through which much of the utility for the modern internet and broader social interactions will occur. The term itself is ripped right from fiction—the "metaverse" was just such a virtual world, which was a centerpiece in *Snow Crash*, though the underlying idea is becoming quite real.

The metaverse is often positioned as a component of a separate but related topic among technologist and futurist in the form of "Web 3.0," the next iteration of the internet that calls for decentralization of information, typically via trustless verification enabled by blockchain. From both a commercial and practical standpoint, this can be understood as a rejection of the "walled gardens" of "Web 2.0," which is often characterized by the rise of user-generated content through networked social platforms such as Facebook. By facilitating (and containing) these exchanges, internet platforms under the aegis of companies like Google/Alphabet and Facebook/Meta amassed profound influence (and accrued a tremendous amount of revenue).

In this light two things are clear: The intentions of Facebook, now Meta, in this direction are hinged on maintaining influence and relevance in an eventual shift from Web 2.0 to Web 3.0, because the metaverse as an idea has been wedded tightly to this future vision of the internet. As a result, the burgeoning conversation around the metaverse has, at a minimum, dramatically expanded the conversation around virtual worlds beyond the domain of gaming. In having a chapter devoted to the future of gaming through the lens of the metaverse, the point is not to portray the metaverse as the eventual and only outcome for the future of gaming. Rather, as has been a consistent theme throughout the book, understanding and fluency in gaming and game players will be a necessary competency for potentially any business or other organization needing to interact with massive groups of consumers. The metaverse provides a reasonably clear blueprint as to how this can unfold for the internet, one that may be traversed in ways that are closer to a game play experience than scrolling a screen. Understanding how to integrate with these environments, and the need state of individuals there, is as vital to short-term executions in gaming as to potential long-term ramifications for human interactivity in virtual worlds, given the long history of these worlds in gaming.

Throughout this book we've already touched on a number of important themes that have bearing on short-term interactions and integrations in gaming which are also relevant to the future state of gaming and a potential metaverse:

- The business of gaming is complex, volatile, and an extraordinarily difficult blend of art and technology that modern companies such as Meta are only just now beginning to reconcile with.
- Gaming represents a particularly provocative form of participatory media, that has a multitude of positive and negative effects for intermediary forces, but largely still encapsulates a community that is highly invested, finds identity within gaming, and in many cases (via modding or otherwise) seeks to be part of building it.
- The psychology of game experiences is unique relative to other forms of media. This can assuage concerns that persistent virtual worlds will turn human society into a mass of cyber

zombies, but it also presents a number of practical challenges for both the literal creation of these worlds and the ways in which outside entities can interact with them meaningfully.

- The worlds of work and play have already blurred in many cases—certainly in the case of professional game play (e.g., esports), but also via streaming and other mechanisms through which gaming has been formulated as an experience beyond the act of game play.

- Gaming has benefited immensely from reducing the levels of esoteric knowledge required to onboard new fans into gaming (the rise of casual games, the simplicity of early arcade games, etc.). As it stands, navigating complex 3D worlds is among the most esoteric types of knowledge within gaming and often more germane to "traditional" gamers, but the potential for mimetic interfaces via VR or AR provides a road to a similar streamline for more mass adoption.

- We've long used video games as a mechanism through which we contextualize new technology, be it personal computers, televisions, or mobile phones. The prospect of core mechanisms of interaction being founded within virtual worlds means that games will likely be the context through which consumers seek to understand this shift, which is convenient, given that (as noted) for the most part the "metaverse" as it exists now is almost entirely within the world of gaming.

In short, we will address future directions and trends for the gaming industry through the lens of metaverse not because metaverse is an eventuality, but rather because the metaverse as it exists now is a set of ideas that are direct antecedents of gaming or are closely related to gaming. It also allows us to apply the lessons necessary to integrating with gaming and understanding the gaming ecosystem to an even broader set of use cases. In doing so, the intention is to not downplay the importance of some of these potential future technologies or paths in isolation or neglect of their own potential, but rather to provide context on their utility and potential in relation to one another using the metaverse as a foundation.

For whatever opinion one may have of the potential or viability of the metaverse, it represents a profound consolidation of deeply human factors relating to identity, ownership, embodiment, socialization, and consumption. It's potentially as grand as a technological mirror for the entirety of the human experience. If it feels silly to base nothing less than the future of the internet on something as frivolous as gaming, it's worthwhile to note that we've learned much about epidemiology[3] and corporate subterfuge[4] from MMO games. Even the ways human biases can be activated (as noted earlier) have been studied by something as simple as virtual avatars in games spaces.[5] However, what is often lost in the various conversations around the metaverse is that the very pieces of fiction that have lit our imaginations towards building a future that includes these virtual worlds describe them as … not very awesome places. Not entirely unlike the broader world of gaming, some know-how and understanding can potentially go a long way to building and integrating with these developing futures in a smart and safe way.

Windows to New Worlds: Virtual, Augmented, and Mixed Reality

To the same extent that the depictions of gaming noted above tend to all gravitate towards the concept of virtual worlds, virtual reality (VR) headsets and peripherals have long been described as the de facto window to these worlds. In some respects, the concepts of "VR" and "metaverse" have become synonymous in the ongoing discourse concerned with the future of the internet. Not entirely unlike gaming, even the most future-facing technologies such as VR have long histories, in this case one that can be traced back nearly as far as the concept of recording images has existed more generally. From stenographic pictures in the early 1800s to flight simulators in the early 1900s, using technology to alter our perceptions of reality and bring forth the feeling that we are immersed in a world not our own has a long history.

The first head-mounted display that conforms more to our expectations of modern virtual reality can be fairly credited to Morton Heilig's Telesphere Mask in the 1960s, though once again modern fiction did much of the lifting to bring the concept to a wider audience, such as Stephen King's *Lawnmower Man* in 1992.[6] It was around this same time that consumer applications in gaming began to pick up steam, ranging from the ill-fated Nintendo Virtual Boy[7] to more recent entrants such as Oculus (notably owned by Facebook/Meta). However, despite the occasionally hyperbolic claims attached to these technologies among marketers and technologists, adoption remains relatively low. As recently as October 2021 the install rate of VR headsets on popular PC gaming platform Steam was just 1.85 percent.[8]

Though adoption of VR continues to expand,[9] the relative malaise around VR among game players is due to a number of important factors to consider. First, these headsets come at considerable cost and often require a powerful gaming PC or console to facilitate the experience (outside of offerings such as the Oculus Quest series of headsets by Facebook/Meta, which is a standalone VR system). Second, the number of gaming titles that require VR, particularly for big gaming franchises, is relatively low. Third and perhaps most importantly, for the most part, VR technology as it exists now doesn't always provide a better experience than what can be experienced on a flat screen. While technological layers such as VR can greatly enhance our capability to establish spatial presence/immersion in a game,[10] they are not strictly necessary—smart design and comparatively better-fidelity visuals on highly tuned gaming monitors or TVs can provide enough visual detail to facilitate deep spatial presence. More simply, the ROI for using often expensive and cumbersome gear just isn't high enough relative to the game experience pay-out, at least as it stands now.

Related concepts such as augmented reality (AR) and mixed reality (MR) present different, less all-encompassing (and therefore, less burdensome from a technology standpoint) ways in which virtualization of worlds can be achieved. AR allows for an augmented technological layer to be placed in real time across the real world via images, graphics, sounds, or other media that are accessible via viewing devices such as a phone (Snapchat has a deep bench of "cameras" and "lenses" that implement AR features) or specialized glasses. From allowing for fitness stats to be viewed in our fields of vision during exercise[11] to dragons landing on the Flatiron building as an innovative marketing stunt,[12] AR doesn't create entire virtual worlds for individuals to navigate so much as introduce virtual elements to the real world.

Mixed reality is a more nuanced take on AR. This technology falls a little closer on the continuum to VR, in that virtual elements are overlaid on the real world that interact with the user and the real world around the virtual element. *Pokémon Go* is perhaps the most famous example of mixed reality, in which players traverse the real world to capture Pokémon superimposed on real locations through their mobile phones, and combated them with other Pokémon at "gyms" geo-anchored to locations in the real world.

The advantage that AR and MR have relative to VR (there are other acronyms we could throw in here for fun if these three aren't enough, including XR or "extended reality," which is a bit of an umbrella term for the core concepts here) is that they overcome the primary adoption barrier to VR—they are readily and easily accessible through more affordable or ubiquitous devices. Does that mean that the future of VR is to become more like AR or MR? Not quite—these technologies serve very distinct potential use cases. The more likely scenario is continued convergence towards:

1. VR experiences that are cheaper, which include a large library of content, and require less cumbersome and higher-quality gear (in terms of the fidelity of visuals, reliance on outside technology such as PCs or consoles, etc.) than what is currently available.

2. AR and MR experiences that continue to hinge on ubiquitous technology but provide more valuable experiences to the end user (e.g., reasons to view an environment via AR that serve some utility).

If the metaverse is to be a virtual world experienced via VR, the same challenge to VR tech today must be posed—what value can the consumer extract from the experience that is better than a flat screen to justify the more obtrusive technological layer? AR and MR may serve as steppingstones for more mainstream consumers not acquainted with the comparatively more complex and specialized equipment for VR, though either way the potential for our everyday lives to include complete or partial technological overlays is gaining increased momentum.

One of the more considerable precursors for wider VR adoption noted above is allowing for usage of these devices without reliance on an outside device such as a PC or console to render the complex 3D visuals that typify VR. The potential to "outsource" heavy computational tasks from local devices therefore has immense ramifications for VR, if not gaming more generally. The emergence of cloud gaming and improvements in mobile high-speed internet provide a viable path to a solution.

A Game for Every Screen: Cloud and 5G

Casual games brought millions into gaming through two important factors: game play design and sensibilities that were appealing to audiences beyond "traditional" game fans, and the prevalence of these games on ubiquitous devices such as mobile phones. One of the key threads running through any discussion of metaverse and related technologies such as VR/AR is that the relative value that these technologies provide must be considered in relation to the barriers of entry for the experience. In this way, cloud gaming and the potential for high-speed mobile data provide an important solve for many current and future game experiences in that they theoretically allow for complex experiences common to more traditional games (or, say, a 3D-rendered metaverse) to basically any viewing screen or device.

The underlying technologies are complex, but the idea is simple—cloud gaming offloads to a server the heavy computational lifting required to (say) render a 3D environment rather than requiring a local device (a phone, computer, or game console) be powerful enough to render the experience. In theory, game experiences that might have otherwise required an expensive and specialized game console or high-end PC can be played on any given mobile phone or other internet-connected device (smart TVs, etc.).

Like VR, the concept of cloud gaming isn't new. Ill-fated endeavors such as OnLive attempted to crack the cloud gaming problem upwards of a decade ago.[13] Even more recent endeavors such as Google's Stadia will encounter a myriad of challenging technical issues to create a seamless game experience,[14] but much of the core challenges relate to access to high-speed internet. Unlike countries such as South Korea, the United States has somewhat lagged (pun intended) in the proliferation of high-speed internet.[15] This represents a challenge to existing infrastructure that is partially solved by mobile internet technologies such as 5G.

Intuitively enough, 5G stands for the "fifth generation" of mobile data networks. This developing generation of mobile internet is noteworthy as it is the first that has the potential to match or beat comparable "high speed" internet via traditional internet providers, (though with eventual plans to reach significantly faster speeds).[16] For applications in the home, it allows for high-speed internet in areas that were previously not able to be serviced due to poor or nonexistent infrastructure. This technology also enables similar experiences to, in theory, be available outside of the home given that it is mobile, broadcast internet. The applications for AR and MR as technologies that currently have high utilization outside the home and "on the go" is obvious. Beyond that, the fact that our working definition of "casual" games, as in ones that have enough flexibility to be weaved into opportune moments of everyday life, can be expanded to include virtually any game type on a mobile phone (or other devices capable to tapping into 5G) is significant, insofar that almost any game experience has the potential to be "casual" by allowing for any game experience to be accessed virtually anywhere. This has knock-on effects such as improving the viability and scale of the budding mobile esports scene[17] (in itself an exciting future direction for gaming and esports), but also the feasibility of bringing complex 3D environments à la most visions of the metaverse to every home (or where applicable outside of the home, everywhere).

The rise of gaming and esports owes much to the proliferation of the consumer internet. As the availability and quality of this access expands so too will the potential for gaming experiences. In the near term, this allows for exciting possibilities regarding the ease in accessing extremely rich gaming experiences (and potentially competing within them). Further on, the normalization of complex virtualized environments across essentially any device is likely an important milestone for the increased virtualization of our everyday life via the metaverse and related technologies.

Cloud technologies combined with 5G are about the future of accessing digital experiences, untethered by the hardware constraints of personal devices. As noted above, the metaverse as a concept is often wedded to a future "Web 3.0," which is similarly untethered, though in this case from centralized brokers of information such as "walled garden" social networks or game services. One of the paths towards the future that is emerging the quickest, and has the most bearing on gaming, is the relationship between blockchain and digital ownership.

Unblocking Value: Blockchain and NFT

All the technologies addressed here, because they are future looking, are rapidly changing. The world of blockchain, and in particular non-fungible tokens (NFTs) or blockchain games are some that stand apart by shifting seemingly day by day. This is in no small part due to the community-based nature of development within blockchain (decentralization is, after all, entirely the point) coupled with the bullish projections on both gaming and cryptocurrencies at the time this book was written. The result is that a discussion of any specific project or emerging trend will be folly, and as such we'll concentrate on broader trends.

To the uninitiated, the blockchain represents a digital ledger where ownership of goods and information can be independently verified instead of relying on any given brokering person or organization to verify (such as a bank, in the case of currencies). As it pertains to gaming, the utilization of cryptocurrencies both for more traditional game transactions or as the de facto currency of the metaverse are some of the most direct applications of blockchain technology.

However, either potentiality has less overall impact on the trajectory of gaming as it pertains to design or distribution so much as giving game transactions or game-adjacent economies a wider berth of currencies (aside from traditional money). A more fundamental shift in game design and the composition of game audiences comes from the potential of NFTs and a related game paradigm called "play to earn."

NFTs are a reasonably complex topic that we won't do justice to here in a few paragraphs, so at the risk of being overly simplistic their main draw in gaming is that they allow a means of ownership of digital assets that can be asserted outside of a centralized ecosystem (e.g., the server of an individual game or service), thereby allowing for the asset to be potentially monetized and resold beyond the confines of a game system, and/or allowing for recurrent income through resale of the asset. More simply, though ownership of digital assets has long existed in the world of gaming (such as the licenses to games or other "items," which are tradable on platforms like Steam), the intervention of NFTs is that the ownership of the asset isn't confined to any given server or platform, and therefore "real value" can be extracted.

While this is a promising future where game play allows for more tangible financial benefits to players, it's also rife with a number of challenges at this time.[18] First and foremost is interoperability between systems—yes, one might be able to extract an item out of a given game environment or ecosystem, but can that same item actually be used or carry value within another system? How do game designers balance a nearly infinite array of items with varying power levels and aesthetics? Various efforts such as Loot (for adventurers)[19] or Forte[20] are attempting to create shared protocols and platforms to ease the process of game development around NFTs, though this will remain an incredibly tricky technological and design problem for some time. Interoperability is also a significant challenge for the metaverse more generally— the internet as it exists now relies on a series of shared languages and protocols that have not, as it stands, been established for the metaverse or Web 3.0 (though various game engines have been proposed as a starting point, which we will discuss at the close of this chapter).

One of the areas within the broader gaming landscape where NFTs have picked up the most traction is in the proliferation of NFT-enabled "play to earn" games. As the name entails, these are games where earning real money (often in the form of cryptocurrencies) can come through the course of game play. Not unlike ownership of digital items, the potential to earn money through games is not necessarily new—grey or black market activities such as "gold farming" (where individuals accrue game currencies to sell back to players for real money)[21] in MMOs like *World of Warcraft* has been an issue as long as internet-connected games have existed. The MMO *Entropia* was among the first to incorporate legitimate earnings within the core game play,[22] though the application of cryptocurrency as the monetary system allows for significantly more flexibility from a regulatory standpoint than games like *Entropia* that leverage traditional currency.

The primary benefit of NFTs and blockchain in gaming, in theory, is that it allows for players to extract real value and (also in theory) a more equitable relationship between players and publishers. This too, at least in its current form, is not without challenges—not the least of which is the deep amount of cynicism towards these technologies from traditional game fans. An announcement that hinted at NFT functionality in the gaming-centric chat platform Discord was met with what amounted to open revolt.[23] The overt focus on commercialization and earning from games has yielded a scenario where, as this time, most NFT games aren't really compelling games so much as microeconomic simulators that come quite close to the much-derided concept of "pay to win" games (where a player with a big bankroll can accrue a material advantage over another).[24]

That said, we've already addressed the problems with gate keeping among the traditional "gamer" community in earlier chapters. The pushback in this case may not amount to much if, not unlike mobile "casual" games, these "play to earn" titles are merely expanding the scope of gaming and the definition of a game fan. It may even be the case that NFT-enabled play-to-earn games create a new mechanism for professionalization in gaming apart from performative channels such as esports or streaming. In other words, blockchain and NFTs may simply be a new, differentiated, and parallel classification of games built around the design freedoms blockchain affords beyond the current model of game production, and a new caste of game players where professionalization (earning) is more embedded in the play experience than simple leisure.

While the core concept of a Web 3.0 is built around decentralization that is largely facilitated by blockchain, the immediate applications to the metaverse by means of increased and differential systems of digital ownership are noteworthy. While a path is presented in terms of how to make ownership of digital items flexible and transferable, it also brings to light one of the core problems related to a concept like the metaverse—how to have assets and items render and work between innumerable virtual worlds built by innumerable different actors. The challenges vs. the potential of these technologies, relative to the value that they can provide to consumers, will continue to be the central point of contention for the future of these technologies both within gaming and as it pertains to the metaverse, a concept that we will return to again in closing.

Ready Player You: Conclusions and Implications

The future of gaming is thus one that potentially involves increased adoption of interfaces that allow deeper immersion à la VR, are decentralized and contain flexible and enduring ownership of digital goods, and ride on the crest of extremely fast data speeds where complex computational tasks are carried out via "cloud" servers rather than by localized environments. The sum of these parts equates to a whole that is very close to the emerging concept of the metaverse—a virtual 3D world that can be traversed not entirely unlike a VR game, which replaces much of what we understand to be the internet as it exists today.

Quite a leap. However, while the conversation around metaverse and related technologies has spiked, the reality of this vision is almost certainly still decades away. What currently exists as the "metaverse" today is largely (you guessed it) game environments—*Roblox, Fortnite*, and other semipersistent virtual worlds are the current exemplars and sandboxes for what may emerge as the metaverse. Epic Games, the creators of *Fortnite* and the Unreal game engine (which may be one of the unifying infrastructures of the metaverse) has already created a bold vision for what the metaverse should be.[25] As a result, the conversation around the importance of metaverse has raised the stakes for truly understanding gaming, although the hype carries the risk of eager marketers and decision makers glossing over this important step (not including you, dear reader, assuming you've made it this far … and have presumably not skipped all the other chapters in this book).

The risks associated with wanton, albeit uniformed, enthusiasm is quite high. John Carmack (the same Carmack that revolutionized PC gaming, was one of the fathers of *DOOM*, and subsequently became the CTO of Oculus) warns of "architectural astronauts" who will wax eloquent about possibilities without understanding how any of the underlying technologies actually work.[26] If you pick up a few ideas from this book, let one of them be that when John Carmack says something about gaming or virtual worlds, we'd do well to listen.

However, before we broach anything as grand as an actual metaverse, we'll see a number of advancements along the lines of the technologies discussed here. As noted, we'll see increasingly large groupings of technology companies become more invested in gaming, either for the sake of creating games themselves or buttressing their capabilities for creating virtual worlds. Most notably in the world of entertainment, Netflix made good on disclosure that it was games like *Fortnite* that were their biggest competitor rather than HBO, based on the amount of attention being monopolized by games such as *Fortnite*, by getting into gaming themselves.[27]

In this respect, the near future of gaming is … more gaming. However, gaming and its antecedents are quickly becoming formative to foundational ways in which humans can interrelate and share information in the future. Understanding these worlds and these audiences will become the differentiator between businesses that make this transition successfully vs. those that fail, or at the very least those that can separate fact from fiction.

Chapter 11

Conclusion

Point of No Return

D etermining when you are near the end of a video game, particularly those with broader, more sprawling narratives, has
become a fair bit easier in modern games. Many introduce what is
colloquially known as a "point of no return"—this is where the player
(and their avatar) advances the narrative to the point that the lead up
to the conclusion of the game kicks off in earnest, ending only in the
roll of the credits. Modern games have adopted a number of more
or less subtle cues at the point of no return—anything from in-game
characters telling the player they should "finish up other business"
before proceeding, to less elegant but very direct prompts from the
game UI asking the player to confirm if they would like to continue.

Players have a choice—they can forgo saving the world/gal-
axy/whatever for a while to finish up other tasks, collect various
MacGuffins, and power themselves up for the climatic ending, or
charge headlong into the final moments of the game. Either way, it
is a false choice—in many of these same games various iterations of
"New Game+" exist (where upon completion of the game, the player
can go through it again on different terms) or DLCs can extend the
narrative sometimes indefinitely. The story and journey never really
end, even after the ominously titled point of no return.

You may see where I'm going with this—we've reached our own
point of no return. We're heading to the conclusion of this story arc,

but one that will continue beyond the pages here. The influence of gaming has broached beyond entertainment, and its impact on the construction of virtual worlds, social connectivity, competitive entertainment, or simply existing as mass-consumed media remains in very early stages. What was presented here was the start, enough to get interested parties towards this newly developing game (hopefully with a plus!), but it would be folly to consider this journey at an end.

How do we proceed past this point such that we aren't compelled to circle back and finish any insights (should we choose not to)? Let's review:

> In Chapter 2 we learned that gaming helps us understand new technologies. Many of our biases against it are rooted in moral panics defined by older generations unwilling or unable to understand the pastime of younger ones, spurred in part by an initial economic focus on young men. As those economics became unsustainable due to the rising costs of advanced game production, the proliferation of gaming has risen due to both more accessible technology and design to make game types for virtually everyone, in ways that could be threaded into everyday life.

> What constitutes a game fan had changed, and in Chapter 3 we tore down the incredibly durable conception of what a gamer was, by understanding the influence of moral panics on public perception. The "othering" of gamers by the media fostered a tendency to calcify the gamer identity among game players at the time (young men), who in turn "othered" those wishing to enter the domain of gaming—by exhibiting extreme tendencies towards ownership and participatory culture. The gamer exists, but it's a small part of the population that drums

up most of the negative connotations around the larger gaming fandom. Investment, ownership, and the highly affective nature of the medium mean that the psychology of these spaces is somewhat unique, and should be handled with care when introducing new elements (be it ads, technology, messages, or otherwise).

We addressed the more problematic or concerning issues around the psychology and culture of gaming in Chapter 4, where we tackled issues of brand safety and representation in gaming through the lens of common concerns related to violence, addiction, and toxicity. We found that scientific consensus on games leading towards addictive or violent behaviors is incredibly mixed and largely blown out of proportion by moral panics, and all sides of the game community are incentivized to stamp out issues of toxicity, which is in part rooted in threated identity by the growth of the gaming umbrella, particularly among women. The drawing power of games (and therefore, their value to marketers) should not be overly conflated with their potential for abuse.

Having established a platform for understanding game play, Chapter 5 addressed immediate opportunities in gaming, with a focus on advertising, partnerships, and advergaming. The scope and desired audience must be balanced against development needs and time, with the understanding that outside interactions are partially funding the gaming ecosystem as it exists now. Creating value to the player and not disrupting the game play or game environment are paramount, as is an empathetic approach to working with game developers and a level-set on what manner of opportunities are more turnkey (such as advertising) versus requiring significant partnership. The disruptiveness of an integration carries a price tag in value that can be given back to the player—no opportunities are impossible, but a narrower set is economically viable as things currently stand.

We transitioned to the broader phenomenon of gaming viewership in Chapter 6, starting with esports. New, evolving, and innovative business models in esports trail viewership that is still very much growing and quite unique in experience relative to viewing other traditional sports. The legacy of gaming being the domain of young men, and disproportionately those with adequate wealth to participate, forms a persisting problem of representation in the industry that bears consideration and is only partially offset by opportunities prevalent in game streaming.

We jumped into the history of esports in Chapter 7, with an emphasis on the social, cultural, and technological factors that have shaped the trajectory of the industry. While esports have a number of parallels to traditional sports, which provides a road map towards understanding, it is differentiated by its complicated relationship with traditional media (resulting in at least one industry crash) and rise to prominence via new mechanisms for broadcasts such as game streaming. This has shaped the prevailing business models around esports organizations, which are predominately digital and lean towards emerging trends such as influencer marketing to funnel much-needed revenue into developing businesses.

The focus was widened in Chapter 8 to discuss game streaming more generally, wherein we find that virtually any game can be an esport of sorts, and game streaming as a vocation is both a mechanism to inject money into the esports ecosystem and a cause of strain for content creators when work and play are combined. This relationship bears due consideration in

Chapter 9, where we explored opportunities in game viewing across esports and streaming, falling largely along the lines of advertisements, sponsorships, and leveraging gaming talent for the purposes of content or influencer marketing. Not unlike gaming, a wide palette is open, though often in direct negotiation with a variety of complex stakeholders ranging from game studios to talent, with differing levels of influence and possibilities that some degree of insider information can help navigate.

Chapter 10 adopted a future-looking view, using the concept of metaverse as an organizing principal to discuss the possibilities afforded by VR/AR, cloud, 5G, Blockchain, and other emerging and influential tech that both have applications in gaming (and in many cases are direct heirs to the legacy of gaming). As a result, the near-term applications and potentials of these technologies will be heavily gaming-centric, which has the combined effect of positioning gaming as both one of the most valuable ecosystems for contextualizing this technology (which as discussed in the history of gaming, has been a common thread since the advent of video games) and understanding their potential beyond gameplay.

Recent years have demonstrated an increasing array of companies signaling interest in gaming—Netflix has notably turned to gaming as a potential to add additional value to a potentially saturated marketplace.[1] The influence of ideas such as the metaverse will yield a number of visions that (sadly) won't look a whole lot different from game platforms such as *Playstation Home* or *Second Life*, due in part to a reluctance to contend with gaming and the lessons it can provide from a long history of virtual worlds. Enthusiasm around the concept of the metaverse and Web 3.0 more generally will have the effect of increasing the number of organizations interested in building virtual worlds (it's entirely possible that familiarity with game engines will become a must-have skill in nongaming dedicated technology companies). Whether it be more direct game offerings or one that is more tangentially related, gaming is exerting influence beyond media habits.

As offered in the opening chapter of this book, our newly established understanding of gaming has the potential to pay dividends beyond appreciating the technology and landscape. Game fans themselves, complete with their multifaceted motivations and unique orientations towards gaming, will be profoundly instructive towards the reception of any number of new technologies. This is due not only to the fact that household decision makers are increasingly comprised of generations who have grown acculturated with gaming and see their consumption of this media no different from (say) watching a movie or listening to music, but that gaming has been media where direct participation and community involvement to build the ecosystem has been present since its earliest days. Before there was "UGC" in video or social platforms, there were mods in video games—entirely new experiences being built on top of others, occasionally eclipsing the popularity of the game it was created from. Technologists will look to the future of phenomenon like Web 3.0 and extol the virtues of this technology being community built—gaming is a community with, and aptitude for, building weaved into its DNA. Fans can be described as early adopters of new media platforms, who often endeavor to gain control of means of cultural production,[2] and this is true for gaming fans through acts ranging from game modding to building in platforms like *Minecraft* or *Roblox*, but one could go so far as to claim they are in actuality early adopters to larger technological forces and trends that are only now becoming more apparent.

The influence of gaming fans on gaming can thus not be understated, but it's a distinction that will blur in coming years—not due to any shifts in the extent to which gaming fans influence gaming media, but to broader trends where "gamer" as a category won't itself be an oddity. There are no small number of more or less convincing arguments out there which make the claim that "everyone is a gamer," the shift is that everyone being a gamer in this case is not a logical "gotcha" for executives who have *Solitaire* installed on their iPhone but a more fundamental cultural shift. If we think about the poorly defined notion of a "gamer" being one who primarily consumes games as part of their media diet, the uniqueness of this phenomenon will continue to slip.[3] The act of gaming and its antecedents are becoming demystified, which is of course a not so subtle goal of this very work.

The potential for a gaming-centric future will elicit a broad range of potential fears. The advent of social media and computerized interaction led prominent thinkers such as Sherry Turkle to paint stark futures of life lived through a screen, where virtual interaction slipped from being "better than nothing" to "better than anything."[4] The thought of living our lives in increasingly virtualized worlds has stoked these very same fears—depending on your point of view, we're either amidst, or on the precipice of, another moral panic (and here you were thinking all those folks who cast down gaming and rock music before were short-sighted and culturally backwards!) as we seek to understand the possibilities of our world lived as life not on, but within, the screen. Not unlike social media, the debates on harm vs. good enabled by these technologies will not be settled overnight. What is different this time is the example social media present towards the potential outcomes of these new technologies, both awesome and terrible. This is the fundamental shift in the conversation that is driving the development of Web 3.0 vs. Web 2.0—how do we not fall prey to mistakes of our information superhighway past?

And yet we are very much in danger of doing so. If we are to believe that the metaverse is the future of communication and information sharing, how it is largely described at this time (inclusive of organizations seminal to the proliferation of social media) is a world perfect for commercialization but less so for creativity. It's an alluring fantasy of control over virtually every commercial decision one can make,[5] because virtual goods can be endlessly made and their raw components extracted from naught but an idea. For virtual worlds to interlink as promised by the vision of the metaverse, rules and standards need to be in place—paraphrasing famed game developer Raph Koster—standards set a limit to creativity. The problem with these scenarios (if not the development of Web 3.0 more generally) is the same one that was prevalent in the development of Web 2.0—technological determinism. We'll put the needs and possibilities of the technology before the needs of the humans.

But it doesn't have to be this way, and this is where our newfound awareness and insight can come into play. We should not let our ambitions to rapidly commercialize these spaces and put literal stakes in virtual ground set the tone and standards for the potentials afforded by these new technologies. Many of those chasing the dream of the metaverse look at it as an awesome fantasy described by works such as *Snow Crash* or *Ready Player One* without the awareness that both works are satires of the evils of capitalism. Beyond the superficial, the fictional works the metaverse draws inspiration from are largely bleak visions for the future.

Intervention in an experience that evokes deep levels of immersion, and to where the consumer feels deep ownership, provokes considerations that are not dissimilar whether it be a game or more generalized virtual world. From this near-term example we can gain an appreciation of the unique psychology that this evokes, and the necessity for value creation proportional with the level of disruption that may be implanted in these experiences. We can understand that what makes competition compelling is as true in a virtual arena as in a real one, and play can become serious work that fundamentally shifts our conceptions of play. Gaming, whether being played or viewed, is a special form of media because the participant is fully at the center of it. Moreover, it's the only form of media that allows for the participant to walk in the shoes of another, share a common goal, or challenge with someone they have never met, and form deeply multifaceted bonds with others regardless of barriers of time and space.

In this sense, gaming is a deeply human way that we use technology, because the act of play is fundamental to the human experience. Building technologies that crib from gaming without humanist consideration is missing this point in a stunning manner. If we set out to learn how to operate businesses within gaming environments it is my hope that you feel that this endeavor is successful, but the broader possibilities that the lessons here afforded may merely be the start of something even bigger.

So, to tie up the gaming metaphor we opened with, we've reached the end with a new vantage point for beginning a slightly more difficult albeit familiar game. The only question left is whether you would like to play again?

Notes

Chapter 1 Introduction

1. Jonathan Stringfield, "Marketing 3.0: Getting Ahead of the Metaverse," Campaign US, January 11, 2022, https://www.campaignlive.com/article/marketing-30-getting-ahead-metaverse/1737212.
2. Tom Wijman, "Global Games Market to Generate $175.8 Billion in 2021; Despite a Slight Decline, the Market Is on Track to Surpass $200 Billion in 2023," NewZoo, May 6, 2021, https://newzoo.com/insights/articles/global-games-market-to-generate-175-8-billion-in-2021-despite-a-slight-decline-the-market-is-on-track-to-surpass-200-billion-in-2023/.
3. Box Office Mojo Yearly Box Office Revenue, https://www.boxofficemojo.com/year/.
4. IFPI, "IFPI Issues Global Music Report 2021," March 23, 2021, https://www.ifpi.org/ifpi-issues-annual-global-music-report-2021/.
5. Electronic Software Association, "2021 Essential Facts About the Video Game Industry," 2021, https://www.theesa.com/resource/2021-essential-facts-about-the-video-game-industry/.

Chapter 2 Tricks Your TV Can Do

1. Michael Z. Newman, *Atari Age: The Emergence of Video Games in America* (Cambridge, MA: MIT Press, 2017), 12.
2. Pete Etchells, *Lost in a Good Game: Why We Play Video Games and What They Can Do for Us* (London: Icon Books Ltd., 2020), 18.
3. Christopher A. Paul, *Free-to-Play: Mobile Video Games, Bias, and Norms* (Cambridge, MA: MIT Press, 2020), 2.
4. Newman, *Atari Age*, 26.

199

5. Charles Paradis, "Insert Coin to Play: Space Invaders and the 100-yen Myth," *The Numismatist* (March 2014).

6. Newman, *Atari Age*, 47–49.

7. Ibid., 51.

8. Edna Mitchell, "The Dynamics of Family Interaction Around Home Video Games," *Marriage & Family Review* 8, no. 1–2 (October 26, 2018), 121–135, doi: 10.1300/J002v08n01_10.

9. Ralph J. Watkins, "A Competitive Assessment of the U.S. Video Game Industry," United States International Trade Commission, Washington, DC, March 1984.

10. Newman, *Atari Age*, 153.

11. Ibid., 187.

12. "The Great 1980s Dungeons & Dragons Panic," BBC News, April 11, 2014, https://www.bbc.com/news/magazine-26328105.

13. Joost van Dreunen, *One Up: Creativity, Competition, and the Global Business of Video Games* (New York: Columbia University Press, 2020), 33.

14. Steven L. Kent, *The Ultimate History of Video Games: From Pong to Pokémon and Beyond: The Story Behind the Craze That Touched Our Lives and Changed the World* (New York: Three Rivers Press, 2001), 280.

15. Blake J. Harris, *Console Wars: Sega, Nintendo, and the Battle That Defined a Generation* (New York: HarperCollins Publishers, 2014).

16. "Senator Calls for Warnings on Video Games," *Washington Post*, December 2, 1993, https://www.washingtonpost.com/archive/lifestyle/1993/12/02/senator-calls-for-warnings-on-video-games/74450503-ed9a-4084-9910-b8e65ac6f0cb.

17. Jesper Juul, *A Casual Revolution: Reinventing Video Games and Their Players* (Cambridge, MA: MIT Press, 2010), 2.

18. Arjun Khapal, "Game Consoles Were Once Banned in China. Now Chinese Developers Want a Slice of the $49 Billion Pie," CNBC, August 15, 2021, https://www.cnbc.com/2021/08/16/chinese-games-developers-eye-a-slice-of-49-billion-console-market.html.

19. David Kushner, *Masters of DOOM: How Two Guys Created an Empire and Transformed Pop Culture* (New York: Random House Trade Paperbacks, 2003).

20. Seth Porges, "The True Story Behind the Original Video Game 'Easter Egg' That Inspired 'Ready Player One,'" *Forbes*, December 20, 2017, https://www.forbes.com/sites/sethporges/2017/12/20/the-true-story-behind-the-original-video-game-easter-egg-that-inspired-ready-player-one/?sh=261de2d82976.

21. van Dreunen, *One Up*, 48–52.

22. Celia Pearce, "The Truth About Baby Boomer Gamers: A Study of Over-Forty Computer Game Players," *Games and Culture*, February 13, 2008, https://doi.org/10.1177/1555412008314132.

23. Chris Wright, "A Brief History of Mobile Games: In the Beginning, There Was Snake," Pocket Gamer, March 14, 2016, https://www.pocketgamer.biz/feature/10619/a-brief-history-of-mobile-games-in-the-beginning-there-was-snake.

24. Daniel Starkey, "Dark Souls III Is Brutally Hard, But You'll Keep Playing Anyway," *Wired*, April 4, 2016, https://www.wired.com/2016/04/dark-souls-iii-review/.

25. Hobonichi (ed.), *Ask Iwata: Words of Wisdom from Satoru Iwata Nintendo's Legendary CEO*, trans. Sam Bett (San Francisco: VIZ Media, LLC, 2019).

26. van Dreunen, *One Up*, 81.

27. Adam Smith, "Farmville Dead: Era-Defining Facebook App Killed Off After Once Reaching 80 Million Players," *Independent*, September 29, 2020, https://www.independent.co.uk/life-style/gadgets-and-tech/zynga-farmville-dead-adobe-flash-facebook-b689911.html.

28. Kevin Anderton, "Research Report Shows How Much Time We Spend Gaming [Infographic]," *Forbes*, March 21, 2019, https://www.forbes.com/sites/kevinanderton/2019/03/21/research-report-shows-how-much-time-we-spend-gaming-infographic/?sh=334f77fa3e07.

29. Jesper Juul, "Fear of Failing? The Many Meanings of Difficulty in Video Games," in *The Video Game Theory Reader* 2, ed. Mark J. P. Wolf and Bernard Perron (New York: Routledge, 2009), 237–252.

30. Juul, *A Casual Revolution*, 39–40.

31. Swapna Krishna, "The Case for Launching Easy Mode for Difficult Games," *Wired*, February 10, 2021, https://www.wired.com/story/casual-gamer-control-easy-mode-wait/.

32. Kellen Browning, "How Microsoft Is Ditching the Video Game Console Wars," *New York Times*, June 10, 2021, https://www.nytimes.com/2021/06/10/technology/xbox-games.html.

33. Paul, *Free-to-Play*, 12–13.

34. Tim Harford, "How a Razor Revolutionized How We Pay for Stuff," BBC News, April 10, 2017, https://www.bbc.com/news/business-39132802.

35. van Dreunen, *One Up*, 26.

36. Paul, *Free-to-Play*, 27.

Chapter 3 Why Do We Game?

1. GWI, "The Gaming Playbook: Everything You Need to Know about the Gaming Audience," https://www.gwi.com/reports/the-gaming-playbook.

2. Daniel Muriel and Garry Crawford, *Video Games as Culture: Considering the Role and Importance of Video Games in Contemporary Society* (New York: Routledge, 2018), 42.

3. Henry Jenkins, *Fans, Bloggers, and Gamers: Exploring Participatory Culture* (New York: New York University Press, 2006), 39.

4. Ibid.

5. Ibid., 40.

6. James Newman, *Playing with Videogames* (London: Routledge, 2008).

7. Henry Jenkins, *Convergence Culture: Where Old and New Media Collide* (New York: New York University Press, 2008), 60.

8. Jenkins, *Fans, Bloggers, and Gamers*, 217.

9. Jamie Madigan, *Getting Gamers: The Psychology of Video Games and Their Impact on the People Who Play Them* (Lanham, MD: Rowman & Littlefield, 2016), 67.

10. Paul Tassi, "You'll Be Surprised What Percent of 'Mass Effect' Players Chose Paragon," *Forbes*, February 22, 2020, https://www.forbes.com/sites/paultassi/2020/02/22/youll-be-surprised-what-percent-of-mass-effect-players-chose-paragon/?sh=4f0e15d46cf5.

11. Muriel and Crawford, *Video Games as Culture*, 90.

12. Madigan, *Getting Gamers*, 44.

13. Erich Goode and Nachman Ben-Yehuda, *Moral Panics: The Social Construction of Deviance* (New York: Wiley-Blackwell, 1994).

14. Julian Gamboa, "'Gamer' Label Is Outdated, Says Electronic Arts' VP of Brand," *Adweek*, July 21, 2021, https://www.adweek.com/inside-the-brand/gamer-label-is-outdated-says-electronic-arts-vp-of-brand/.

15. "Gallery of the Gamer," Activision Blizzard Media, https://www.galleryofthegamer.com.

16. Wendy Grossman, *net wars* (New York: NYU Press, 1998).

17. Jenkins, *Fans, Bloggers, and Gamers*, 142.

18. T. L. Taylor, *Watch Me Play: Twitch and the Rise of Game Live Streaming* (Princeton: Princeton University Press, 2018), 232.

19. Richard Bartle, "Hearts, Clubs, Diamonds, Spades: Players Who Suit MUDs," mud.co.uk, April 1996, http://mud.co.uk/richard/hcds.htm.

20. Nick Yee, "Motivations for Play in Online Games," *CyberPsychology & Behavior* 9, no. 6 (2006): 772–775.

21. Richard M. Ryan and Edward L. Deci, "Self-Determination Theory and the Facilitation of Intrinsic Motivation, Social Development, and Well-Being," *American Psychologist* 55, no. 1 (2000).

22. Andrew K. Przybylski, C. Scott Rigby, and Richard M. Ryan, "A Motivational Model of Video Game Engagement," *Review of General Psychology* 14, no. 2 (2010): 154–166.

23. Madigan, *Getting Gamers*, 120.

24. Ibid., 130–131.

25. Werner Wirth, Matthias Hofer, and Holger Schramm, "The Role of Emotional Involvement and Trait Absorption in the Formation of Spatial Presence," *Media Psychology* 15, no. 1 (March 2012): 19–43.

26. Muriel and Crawford, *Video Games as Culture*, 123.

27. Nick Yee, *The Proteus Paradox: How Online Games and Virtual Worlds Change Us: And How They Don't* (New Haven: Yale University Press, 2014).

28. Daryl J. Bem, "Self-Perception: An Alternative Interpretation of Cognitive Dissonance Phenomena," *Psychological Review* 74, no. 3 (May 1967): 183–200, doi: 10.1037/h0024835.

29. Nick Yee, Jeremy Bailenson, and Nicolas Ducheneaut, "The Proteus Effect: Implications of Transformed Digital Self-Representation on Online and Offline Behavior," *Communication Research* 36, no. 2 (2009).

30. Madigan, *Getting Gamers*, 6.

31. Yubo Kou and Bonnie Nardi, "Regulating Anti-Social Behavior on the Internet: The Example of League of Legends," University of California, Irvine, February 2013, doi: 10.9776/13289.

Chapter 4 Underworld

1. Roughly paraphrasing Paul, who in turn was referencing Adrienne Shaw, "The Internet Is Full of Jerks, Because the World Is Full of Jerks: What Feminist Theory Teaches Us about the Internet," *Communication and Critical/Cultural Studies* 11, no. 3 (2014): 273–277.

2. Carly A. Kocurek, *Coin-Operated Americans: Rebooting Boyhood at the Video Game Arcade* (Minneapolis: University of Minnesota Press, 2015).

3. Tiffany Hsu, "When Mortal Kombat Came Under Congressional Scrutiny," *New York Times*, March 8, 2018, https://www.nytimes.com/2018/03/08/business/video-games-violence.html.

4. "Senator Calls for Warnings on Video Games," *Washington Post*, December 2, 1993, https://www.washingtonpost.com/archive/lifestyle/1993/12/02/senator-calls-for-warnings-on-video-games/74450503-ed9a-4084-9910-b8e65ac6f0cb.

5. Mike Nizza, "Tying Columbine to Video Games," *The Lede* (blog), July 5, 2007, https://thelede.blogs.nytimes.com/2007/07/05/tieing-columbine-to-video-games.

6. Erich Goode and Nachman Ben-Yehuda, *Moral Panics: The Social Construction of Deviance* (New York: Wiley-Blackwell, 1994).

7. Jamie Madigan, *Getting Gamers: The Psychology of Video Games and Their Impact on the People Who Play Them* (Lanham, MD: Rowman & Littlefield, 2016), 225.

8. Andrew K. Przybylski, "Who Believes Electronic Games Cause Real World Aggression?" *Cyberpsychology, Behavior, and Social Networking* 17, no. 4 (April 17, 2014): 228–234, doi: 10.1089/cyber.2013.0245.

9. Christopher J. Ferguson and John Colwell, "Understanding Why Scholars Hold Different Views on the Influences of Video Games on Public Health," *Journal of Communication* 67, no. 3 (March 2017): 305–327, https://doi.org/10.1111/jcom.12293.

10. Madigan, *Getting Gamers*, 225–226.

11. Kimberly M. Thompson and Kevin Haninger, "Violence in E-rated Video Games," *JAMA Network* 5, no. 286 (August 1, 2001): 591–599. doi:10.1001/jama.286.5.591.

12. Craig A. Anderson et al., "Violent Video Game Effects on Aggression, Empathy, and Prosocial Behavior in Eastern and Western Countries: A Meta-Analytic Review," *Psychological Bulletin* 136, no. 2 (March 2010): doi: 10.1037/a0018251.

13. Craig Anderson et al., "Interactive Effects of Life Experience and Situational Cues on Aggression in Japan and the United States," *Pediatrics* 122, no. 5, 208, doi: 10.1532/peds.2008-1425.

14. Patrick M. Markey, Charlotte N. Markey, and Juliana E. French, "Violent Video Games and Real-World Violence: Rhetoric Versus Data," *Psychology of Popular Media Culture* 4, no. 4 (2015): 277–295.

15. Lawrence Kutner and Cheryl Olson, "Why Kids Play Violent Video Games," in *Grand Theft Childhood: The Suprising Truth about Violent Video Games and What Parents Can Do* (New York: Simon & Schuster, 2008).

16. Pete Etchells, *Lost in a Good Game: Why We Play Video Games and What They Can Do for Us* (London: Icon Books Ltd, 2020), 167.

17. Ibid., 169.

18. Brenda Goh, "Three Hours a Week: Play Time's Over for China's Young Video Gamers," Reuters, August 31, 2021, https://www.reuters.com/world/china/china-rolls-out-new-rules-minors-online-gaming-xinhua-2021-08-30.

19. Mike Snider, "Video Games Can Be a Healthy Social Pastime During Coronavirus Pandemic," *USA Today*, March 28, 2020, https://www.usatoday.com/story/tech/gaming/2020/03/28/video-games-whos-prescription-solace-during-coronavirus-pandemic/2932976001.

20. Celia Hodent, *The Psychology of Video Games* (New York: Routledge, 2021), 78.

21. Nick Yee and Nicholas Ducheneaut, "High-Value Monetizers-De-bunking Assumptions Using Personality Psychology," lecture given at the 2014 Game Developer Conference, San Francisco (March 17, 2014).

22. Jeff Kuznekoff and Lindsey Rose, "Communication in Multiplayer Gaming: Examining Player Responses to Gender Cues," *New Media & Society* 15, no. 4 (2012): 541–556.

23. Christopher A. Paul, *The Toxic Meritocracy of Video Games: Why Gaming Culture Is the Worst* (Minneapolis: University of Minnesota Press, 2018).

24. Kocurek, *Coin-Operated Americans*, 188.

25. Christopher A. Paul, *Free to Play: Mobile Video Games, Bias, and Norms* (Cambridge, MA: MIT Press, 2020), 9.

26. Raph Koster, *Theory of Fun for Game Design*, 2nd ed. (Sebastopol, CA: O'Reilly Media, Inc., 2013).

27. Amanda Cote, "'Casual Resistance: A Longitudinal Case Study of Video Gaming's Gendered Construction and Related Audience Perceptions," *Journal of Communication* 70, no. 6 (December 2020): 819–841, https://doi.org/10.1093/joc/jqaa028.

28. Kyle Orland, "Study: Online Gaming 'Losers' Are More Likely to Harass Women," Ars Technica, July 21, 2015, https://arstechnica.com/gaming/2015/07/study-online-gaming-losers-are-more-likely-to-harass-women/.

29. T. L. Taylor, *Raising the Stakes: E-Sports and the Professionalization of Computer Gaming* (Cambridge, MA: MIT Press, 2012), 120–121.

30. Paul, *Free to Play*, 169.

31. Caitlin Dewey, "The Only Guide to Gamergate You Will Ever Need to Read," *Washington Post*, October 14, 2014, https://www.washingtonpost.com/news/the-intersect/wp/2014/10/14/the-only-guide-to-gamergate-you-will-ever-need-to-read/.

32. Paul, *The Toxic Meritocracy of Video Games*, 118.

33. Paul Tassi, "EA Now Seems Legitimately Terrified of Loot Boxes After 'Battlefront 2,'" *Forbes*, April 17, 2018, https://www.forbes.com/sites/insertcoin/2018/04/17/ea-now-seems-legitimately-terrified-of-loot-boxes-after-battlefront-2/?sh=75aefa9b648e.

Chapter 5 Getting in the Game (without Changing It)

1. Jason Schreier, "Game On: Former PlayStation Chief Muses on the Future of Video Gaming," Bloomberg, September 3, 2021, https://www.bloomberg.com/news/newsletters/2021-09-03/ex-playstation-chief-mulls-future-of-gaming-and-his-new-job.

2. Ian Bogost, *How to do Things with Videogames* (Minneapolis: University of Minnesota Press, 2011), 55.

3. For the purposes of this section, we will consider "advertising" to mean video or static marketing messages.

4. eMarketer provides a reasonably up to date round-up of commonly-cited studies: https://www.emarketer.com/content/us-consumers-appreciate-in-game-ads.

5. Disclosure: This article references an interview with the author, conducting research on behalf of a gaming company: https://www.adexchanger.com/mobile/rewarded-video-the-name-of-the-game-at-king/.

6. IAB, "Opt-In Value Exchange Advertising Playbook for Brands," December 5, 2018, https://www.iab.com/wp-content/uploads/2018/12/Opt-in-Value-Exchange-Advertising-for-Brands-Playbook-FINAL-12-5-18.pdf.

7. Tim Cross, "CTV-Style Ads Are Converting Skeptical Brands to Gaming," *Videoweek*, August 31, 2021, https://videoweek.com/2021/08/31/ctv-style-ads-are-converting-sceptical-brands-to-gaming.

8. Broad references here are pulled from the Interactive Advertising Bureau's Game Advertising Framework: https://www.iab.com/insights/gaming-and-esports-advertising-framework/.

9. Jamie Madigan, *Getting Gamers: The Psychology of Video Games and Their Impact on the People Who Play Them* (Lanham, MD: Maryland: Rowman & Littlefield, 2016), 130–131.

10. Henry Jenkins, *Convergence Culture: Where Old and New Media Collide* (New York: New York University Press, 2006), 88–90.

11. Jody Macgregor, "Mods Restore Crazy Taxi's Analog Controls, Product Placement, and More," *PC Gamer*, August 8, 2021, https://www.pcgamer.com/mods-restore-crazy-taxis-analog-controls-product-placement-and-more.

12. Nick Gillett, "Mercedes Benz Kart Arrives as Free Downloadable Content," *The Guardian*, August 23, 2014 https://www.theguardian.com/technology/2014/aug/23/mario-kart-8-mercedes-benz.

13. Patricia Hernandez, "Fortnite Is Basically a Giant, Endless Advertisement Now: Brands All the Way Down," Polygon, May 23, 2019, https://www.polygon.com/2019/5/23/18635920/fortnite-jumpman-john-wick-marvel-brand-advertisement.

14. Chantal Tode, "Cheerios Rain Down on Angry Birds' Piggies in Limited-Time Integration," Marketing Dive, accessed December 2, 2021, https://www.marketingdive.com/ex/mobilemarketer/cms/news/gaming/21012.html.

15. Jason Schreier, *Blood, Sweat, and Pixels: The Triumphant, Turbulent Stories Behind How Video Games Are Made* (New York: HarperCollins, 2017).

16. Casey O'Donnell, *Developer's Dilemma: The Secret World of Videogame Creators* (Cambridge, MA: MIT Press, 2014).

17. Herman Tulleken, "Four Decades of Advergames: Highlights from the History of Advergames," *Game Developer*, June 13, 2019, https://www.gamedeveloper.com/business/four-decades-of-advergames.

18. Marcy Magiera, "7Up's Videogame Hits the Spot: But Soft-drink Marketer Says the Goal Wasn't Interactive Marketing," *AdAge*, January 10, 1994, https://adage.com/article/news/7up-s-videogame-hits-spot/88781.

19. Erik Kain, "5 Things You Really Need to Know About the KFC Console," *Forbes*, February 26, 2021, https://www.forbes.com/sites/erikkain/2021/02/26/5-things-you-really-need-to-know-about-the-kfc-console/?sh=3ea70d1312dd.

20. Kevin Webb, "I Played KFC's Bizarre Colonel Sanders Dating Game So You Don't Have To," *Business Insider*, September 26, 2019, https://www.businessinsider.com/kfc-dating-game-sim-i-love-you-colonel-sanders-2019-9#youll-be-able-to-choose-from-a-collection-of-conversation-options-to-try-and-win-the-colonels-heart-5.

21. Steven Bellman et al., "The Effectiveness of Advergames Compared to Television Commercials Featuring Advergames," *Computers in Human Behavior*, no. 32 (March 2014): 276–283, https://doi.org/10.1016/j.chb.2013.12.013.

22. Travis Northrop, "Nerf Legends Review," *IGN*, updated December 3, 2021, https://www.ign.com/articles/nerf-legends-review.
23. Sun Joo-Grace Ahn and Jeremy N. Bailenson, "Self-Endorsing versus Other Endorsing in Virtual Environments," *Journal of Advertising* 40, no. 2 (January 2011): 93–106, doi:10.2307/23048707.

Chapter 6 Multiplayer

1. Meilan Solly, "The Best Board Games of the Ancient World," *Smithsonian Magazine*, February 6, 2020, https://www.smithsonianmag.com/science-nature/best-board-games-ancient-world-180974094.
2. Robert B. Zajonc, "Attitudinal Effects of Mere Exposure," *Journal of Personality and Social Psychology* 9, no. 2 (1968): 1–27, https://doi.org/10.1037/h0025848.
3. Andrew K. Przybylski, "Who Believes Electronic Games Cause Real World Aggression?" *Cyberpsychology, Behavior, and Social Networking* 17, no. 4 (April 17, 2014): 228–234, Doi: 10.1089/cyber.2013.0245.
4. NewZoo, "NewZoo's Global Esports and Live Streaming Market Report," April 19, 2022, https://newzoo.com/insights/trend-reports/newzoo-global-esports-live-streaming-market-report-2022-free-version.
5. William Collis, *The Book of Esports* (New York: Rosetta Books, 2020).
6. Michael Gwilliam, "Smash Ultimate & Melee Players Rejoice as Nintendo Finally Reveals Esports Circuit," Dexerto, November 18, 2021, https://www.dexerto.com/smash/smash-ultimate-melee-players-rejoice-as-nintendo-finally-reveals-esports-circuit-1701823/.
7. Aubri Juhasz, "As Esports Take Off, High School Leagues Get in the Game," NPR, January 24, 2020, https://www.npr.org/2020/01/24/798172352/as-esports-take-off-high-school-leagues-get-in-the-game.
8. "The Rise of Collegiate Esports Programs," AthleticDirectorU, https://www.athleticdirectoru.com/articles/the-rise-of-collegiate-esports-programs.
9. Anh Luu et. al., "Reaction Times for Esport Competitors and Traditional Physical Athletes are Faster than Noncompetitive Peers," *Ohio Journal of Science* 121, no. 2 (April 2021): 15–20, https://doi.org/10.18061/ojs.v121i2.7677.

10. T. L. Taylor, *Raising the Stakes: E-Sports and the Professionalization of Computer Gaming* (Cambridge, MA: MIT Press, 2012), 47.

11. Baro Hyun, *Demystifying Esports: A Personal Guide to the History and Future of Competitive Gaming* (Carson City, NV: Lioncrest Publishing, 2020).

12. Taylor, *Raising the Stakes*, 175.

13. Ibid., 235–236.

14. Matt Kamen, "ESL Launches 'Counter Strike: Global Offensive' Women's League," NME, December 21, 2021, https://www.nme.com/news/gaming-news/esl-launches-counter-strike-global-offensive-womens-league-3123886.

15. Jaz Rignall, "Top 10 Highest-Grossing Arcade Games of All Time," *US Gamer*, January 1, 2016, https://www.usgamer.net/articles/top-10-biggest-grossing-arcade-games-of-all-time.

16. Roland Li, *Good Luck Have Fun: The Rise of eSports* (New York: Skyhorse Publishing, 2016), 146.

17. Paul "Redeye" Chaloner, *This Is Esports (and How to Spell it): An Insider's Guide to the World of Pro Gaming* (London: Bloomsbury Publishing PLC, 2020), 117–130.

Chapter 7 Good Luck Having Fun

1. William Collis, *The Book of Esports* (New York: Rosetta Books, 2020).

2. Paul "Redeye" Chaloner, *This Is Esports (and How to Spell It): An Insider's Guide to the World of Pro Gaming* (London: Bloomsbury Publishing PLC, 2020), 35–36.

3. David Kushner's *Masters of Doom: How Two Guys Created an Empire and Transformed Pop Culture* (New York: Random House, 2004) is an excellent and entertaining account of the early days of id Software—the studio behind important titles such as *Wolfenstein 3D*, *DOOM*, and *Quake*.

4. David O'Keefe, "How Blizzard's StarCraft Became South Korea's National Pastime," *The Esports Observer*, October 29, 2018, https://archive.esportsobserver.com/starcraft-ii-esports-essentials.

5. Chaloner, *This Is Esports*, 67.

6. See Dota 2 Prize Pool Tracker (https://dota2.prizetrac.kr/) for a historical and real-time tracker of International and other *Dota* prize pools.

7. This is certainly not a matter that has been completely settled or become less complicated as a function of time—Twitch and the creators on the platform are regularly in conflict with the music industry via DMCA takedowns (https://blog.twitch.tv/en/2020/11/11/music-related-copyright-claims-and-twitch/).

8. Roger Groves, "Robert Kraft Investment in Esports Telling About Millennial Disaffection with Traditional Sports," *Forbes*, July 17, 2017, https://www.forbes.com/sites/rogergroves/2017/07/17/robert-kraft-investment-in-esports-telling-about-millennial-disaffection-with-traditional-sports/?sh=482435f8347f.

9. Jacob Wolf, "Sources: Overwatch League Expansion Slots Expected to Be $30 Million to $60 Million," ESPN, May 10, 2018, https://www.espn.com/esports/story/_/id/23464637/overwatch-league-expansion-slots-expected-30-60-million.

10. Collis, *The Book of Esports*, 85.

11. Rohan Nadkarni, "The Stream Team," *Sports Illustrated*, June 10, 2021, https://www.si.com/tech-media/2021/06/10/daily-cover-faze-clan-kyler-murray-bronny-james.

12. Mike Stubbs, "McDonald's Sponsors FaZe Clan in Major Deal," *Forbes*, August 3, 2021, https://www.forbes.com/sites/mikestubbs/2021/08/03/mcdonalds-sponsors-faze-clan-in-major-deal/?sh=35ca030570cf.

13. Andrew Webster, "Epic Pledges $20 Million for Fortnite Esports in 2021," The Verge, January 19, 2021, https://www.theverge.com/2021/1/19/22239161/fortnite-esports-fncs-prize-pool-2021.

14. Niko Mobile Esports Report, "Special Report: Evolution of Mobile Esports for the Mass Market," Niko Partners report, August 18, 2019, https://nikopartners.com/wp-content/uploads/2019/08/Evolution-of-Mobile-Esports-for-the-Mass-Market.pdf.

Chapter 8 Work to Play and Play to Work

1. Sara Lebow, "Global Time Spent Watching Livestreaming Video Game Content Has Nearly Doubled Since Q1 2020," eMarketer Insider Intelligence,

September 21, 2021, https://www.emarketer.com/content/time-spent-watching-livestreaming-video-game-content-worldwide.

2. T. L. Taylor, *Watch Me Play: Twitch and the Rise of Game Live Streaming* (Princeton: Princeton University Press, 2018), 33.

3. Ibid., 22.

4. Kevin Hitt, "Seth 'Scump' Abner Signed by Oakley as Its First Professional Esports Athlete," *Esports Observer*, March 2, 2021, https://archive.esportsobserver.com/scump-oakley-partnership.

5. Chris Baraniuk, "They Dreamed of Esports Glory: Then Their Bodies Broke Down," *Wired*, October 27, 2010, https://www.wired.co.uk/article/esports-injuries-mental-health.

6. William Collis, *The Book of Esports* (New York: Rosetta Books, 2020), 140.

7. Ian Walker, "*Dragon Quest* Speedrunners Are Roasting Their Classic Consoles to Trigger Glitches: Japanese Speedrunners Say Don't Worry, the Consoles Are Fine," Kotaku, December 28, 2020, https://kotaku.com/dragon-quest-speedrunners-are-roasting-their-classic-co-1845958614.

8. Erica Lenti, "Why Do Gamers Like Speedrunning So Much Anyway?" *Wired*, July 10, 2021, https://www.wired.com/story/why-gamers-love-speedrunning.

9. Alex Miller, "The Games Done Quick Marathon Is More Important than Ever," *Wired*, July 2, 2021, https://www.wired.com/story/games-done-quick-gdq-more-important-than-ever.

10. Paige Leskin, "The Career of PewDiePie, the Controversial 30-Year-Old Video Creator Who Just Returned to YouTube After a 30-Day Hiatus," *Business Insider*, updated March 5, 2021, https://www.businessinsider.com/pewdiepie-youtube-felix-kjellberg-life-career-controversy-2019-9.

11. Lisa Respers France, "Drake and Ninja's 'Fortnite' Battle Sets a New Twitch Record," CNN, updated March 15, 2021, https://www.cnn.com/2018/03/15/entertainment/drake-ninja-fortnite-twitch-battle/index.html.

12. David Marchese, "Teenagers Made Ninja a Gaming Superstar: He Has a Message for Parents," *New York Times*, January 24, 2021, https://www.nytimes.com/interactive/2021/01/25/magazine/ninja-interview.html.

13. Ari Notis, "Twitch Streamers Are Boycotting the Site for a Day to Protest Hate Raids," Kotaku, August 23, 2021, https://kotaku.com/twitch-streamers-are-boycotting-the-site-for-a-day-to-p-1847538808.

14. Taylor, *Watch Me Play*, 40–41.

15. Ibid., 70–71.

16. Rolfe Winkler, Jack Nicas, and Ben Fritz, "Disney Severs Ties with You-Tube Star PewDiePie After Anti-Semitic Posts," *Wall Street Journal*, updated February 14, 2017, https://www.wsj.com/articles/disney-severs-ties-with-youtube-star-pewdiepie-after-anti-semitic-posts-1487034533.

17. Austen Goslin, "Dr. Disrespect Was Banned from E3 for Streaming Inside a Bathroom," Polygon, June 12, 2019, https://www.polygon.com/2019/6/12/18662901/dr-disrespect-banned-e3-twitch-bathroom-stream.

18. Roland Li, *Good Luck Have Fun: The Rise of eSports* (New York: Skyhorse Publishing, 2016), 86.

19. Roger Caillois, *Man, Play, and Games,* trans. Meyer Barash (Urbana: University of Illinois Press, 2001).

20. Oscar Gonzalez, "Twitch Hot Tub Streams Explained: Bikinis, Otters, and Controversies," CNet, May 27, 2021, https://www.cnet.com/news/twitch-hot-tub-streams-explained-bikinis-otters-and-controversy.

Chapter 9 Unbalanced

1. "The Olympics Is a Ratings Flop: Advertisers Don't Care," *The Economist*, August 14, 2021.

2. Adario Strange, "Back from the Dead, G4TV Looks to Cash In on the Gaming Craze It Helped Create," Quartz, October 19, 2021, https://qz.com/2075427/g4tvs-returns-adds-another-major-player-to-esports-media/amp.

3. Fred Backus, "More Americans Say They are 'Cutting the Cord,'" CBS News, April 23, 2021, https://www.cbsnews.com/news/cord-cutting-americans-rising.

4. Christopher Zara, "Cord-Cutting Is Killing the Casual TV Sports Fan," *Fast Company*, September 20, 2021, https://www.fastcompany.com/90678385/cord-cutting-is-killing-the-casual-tv-sports-fan.

5. Joe Drape, "Step Aside, LeBron and Dak, and Make Room for Banjo and Kazooie," *New York Times*, December 19, 2021, https://www.nytimes.com/2021/12/19/sports/esports-fans-leagues-games.html.

6. YouGov, "The Most-Followed Sports Team among American Teen Males Is Actually an Esports Team," November 19, 2021, https://today.yougov.com/topics/technology/articles-reports/2021/11/19/most-followed-sports-team-among-american-teen-male.

7. Sarah Bond, "Yes, Ancient Olympic Athletes Had Sponsorship Deals, Too," *Forbes*, August 10, 2016, https://www.forbes.com/sites/drsarahbond/2016/08/10/how-athletes-have-made-money-off-the-olympics-from-ancient-athens-to-rio/?sh=312eac0168e1.

8. Joost van Dreunen, *One Up: Creativity, Competition, and the Global Business of Video Games* (New York: Columbia University Press, 2020), 200.

9. TJ McCue, "47 Percent of Consumers Are Blocking Ads," *Forbes*, March 19, 2019, https://www.forbes.com/sites/tjmccue/2019/03/19/47-percent-of-consumers-are-blocking-ads/?sh=11e05f062037.

10. Sarah Perez, "Twitch's New Video Ads Can't Be Blocked," *Tech Crunch*, November 2, 2016, https://techcrunch.com/2016/11/02/twitch-starts-selling-its-own-video-ads-says-they-cant-be-avoided-via-ad-blockers.

11. Bijan Stephen, "Twitch Is Running a PSA for People Using Ad-Blockers on the Site, and Nobody's Happy," The Verge, November 3, 2020, https://www.theverge.com/2020/11/3/21547669/twitch-adblock-ublock-midroll-preroll-ads.

12. Billy Studholme, "Activision Blizzard Conducts Research, Finds Esports Fans More Receptive to Advertising," *Esports Insider*, February 16, 2021, https://esportsinsider.com/2021/02/activision-research-esports-receptive-advertising. *Disclaimer: The author was involved in conducting this research.*

13. "NewZoo's Global Esports Live Streaming Market Report," Newzoo, March 9, 2021, https://newzoo.com/insights/trend-reports/newzoos-global-esports-live-streaming-market-report-2021-free-version.

14. Tobias Seck, "Resolving Conflicts of Interest Holds Key to More Revenue," *Sports Business Journal*, August 16, 2021, https://sportsbusinessjournal.com/Journal/Issues/2021/08/16/In-Depth/Esports-conflicts-of-interest.aspx.

15. Marty Strenczewilk, "It's Time for Esports to Stop Idolizing Traditional Sports," *Future*, September 8, 2021, https://future.a16z.com/esports-business-models.

16. For example, the three-year deal between Twitch, ESL, and DreamHack, https://about.eslgaming.com/blog/2020/04/esl-and-dreamhack-enter-streaming-deal-with-twitch.

17. Roland Li, *Good Luck Have Fun: The Rise of eSports* (New York: Skyhorse Publishing, 2016), 157–160.

18. "Grubhub Levels Up in Esports as the Official Food Delivery Partner of the League Championship Series," Grubhub, January 14, 2021, https://media.grubhub.com/media/News/press-release-details/2021/Grubhub-levels-up-in-esports-as-the-Official-Food-Delivery-Partner-of-the-League-Championship-Series/default.aspx; and H. B. Duran, "LCS Names Grubhub as Presenting Partner," *Esports Insider*, January 14, 2021, https://esportsinsider.com/2021/01/lcs-grubhub-partnership.

19. YouGov, "YouGov Game-Changers: The Power of Gaming Influencers," YouGov, 2021, https://commercial.yougov.com/rs/464-VHH-988/images/YouGov_Game-Changers%202021_PART%201.pdf.

20. Nathan Grayson, "The Twitch Hack Revealed Much More than Streamer Salaries: Here Are 4 New Takeaways," *Washington Post*, October 8, 2021, https://www.washingtonpost.com/video-games/2021/10/08/twitch-hack-leak-minimum-wage-pay-hasan.

21. Ed Nightingale, "Twitch Leak Reveals Streamer Earnings and Lack of Diversity," *Eurogamer*, updated October 12, 2021, https://www.eurogamer.net/articles/2021-10-06-twitch-leak-reveals-streamer-earnings-and-lack-of-diversity.

22. Danny Appleford, "100 Thieves Announce Their Collaboration with Gucci," *Upcomer*, July 12, 2021, https://www.upcomer.com/100-thieves-announce-their-collaboration-with-gucci.

23. Alex Hawgood, "Valkyrae Gets a Big Chair in the Gaming World," *New York Times*, April 7, 2021, https://www.nytimes.com/2021/04/07/style/valkyrae-rachell-hofstetter-100-Thieves-Among-Us.html.

24. Jeff Beer, "Faze Clan and McDonald's Drop New Campaign to Encourage Diversity in Gaming," *Fast Company*, November 30, 2021, https://

www.fastcompany.com/90700821/faze-clan-and-mcdonalds-drop-new-campaign-to-encourage-diversity-in-gaming.

25. Bijan Stephen, "Ninja, Shroud, and Other Top Mixer Streamers Are Now Free to Stream on Twitch Again," The Verge, June 22, 2021, https://www.theverge.com/2020/6/22/21298963/ninja-shroud-mixer-facebook-gaming-twitch.

26. Kori Hale, "Esports Heavyweight FaZe Clan Shoots Its $1 Billion IPO Shot Via SPAC Merger," *Forbes*, November 3, 2021, https://www.forbes.com/sites/korihale/2021/11/03/esports-heavyweight-faze-clan-shoots-its-1-billion-ipo-shot-via-spac-merger/?sh=2cd7692f34ef.

27. Sam Weber, "Top Esports Athletes on Social | How Much Can They Make with Social?" Opendorse, May 1, 2020, https://opendorse.com/blog/how-much-can-esports-athletes-earn-on-social-media.

28. Lucy Michaeloudis, "Gaming Influencers: A Step-by-Step Campaign Guide," The Drum, May 19, 2021, https://www.thedrum.com/industry-insights/2021/05/19/gaming-influencers-step-step-campaign-guide.

29. Dani Gibson, "Pokimane Launches Agency to Fix 'Broken' Relationship Between Gamers and Brands," The Drum, October 27, 2021, https://www.thedrum.com/news/2021/10/27/influencer-pokimane-launches-agency-fix-broken-relationship-between-gamers-and.

Chapter 10 Life in the Screen

1. Barbara Ortutay, "In the Middle of a Crisis, Facebook Inc. Renames Itself Meta," AP News, October 28, 2021, https://apnews.com/article/facebook-meta-mark-zuckerberg-technology-business-5ad543ab7780caae435935f0aca9fac6.

2. Kevin Roose, "Facebook Is Now a Mobile Company," Intelligencer, January 30, 2013, https://nymag.com/intelligencer/2013/01/facebook-is-now-a-mobile-company.html.

3. Jhaan Elker, "World of Warcraft Experienced a Pandemic in 2015: That Experience May Help Coronavirus Researchers," *The Washington Post*, April 9, 2020, https://www.washingtonpost.com/video-games/2020/04/09/world-warcraft-experienced-pandemic-2005-that-experience-may-help-coronavirus-researchers.

4. Michael Casey, "Real Economist Learns from Virtual World," *Wall Street Journal*, June 21, 2010, https://www.wsj.com/articles/BL-REB-10618.

5. Nick Yee and Jeremy Bailenson, "The Proteus Effect: The Effect of Transformed Self-Representation on Behavior," *Human Communication Research* 33 (2007): 271–290, https://stanfordvr.com/mm/2007/yee-proteus-effect.pdf.

6. "History of Virtual Reality," Virtual Reality Society, 2017, https://www.vrs.org.uk/virtual-reality/history.html.

7. Graham Flanagan, "The Incredible Story of the 'Virtual Boy'—Nintendo's VR Headset from 1995 That Failed Spectacularly," *Business Insider*, March 26, 2018, https://www.businessinsider.com/nintendo-virtual-boy-reality-3d-video-games-super-mario-2018-3.

8. Steam Hardware Survey, October 2021, https://store.steampowered.com/hwsurvey.

9. Noah Smith, "Virtual Reality Is Starting to See Actual Gains in Games," *Washington Post*, February 4, 2021, https://www.washingtonpost.com/video-games/2021/02/04/virtual-reality-future-games.

10. Jamie Madigan, *Getting Gamers: The Psychology of Video Games and Their Impact on the People Who Play Them* (Lanham, MD: Rowman & Littlefield, 2016), 134.

11. Patrick Liu, "How Augmented Reality Will Transform the Fitness Industry," *TechCrunch*, https://techcrunch.com/sponsor/photonlens/how-augmented-reality-will-transform-the-fitness-industry.

12. Todd Spangler, "'Game of Thrones' Ice Dragon Lands on NYC's Flatiron Building in New Snapchat Lens (Watch)," *Variety*, April 12, 2019, https://variety.com/2019/digital/news/game-of-thrones-snapchat-dragon-flatiron-building-1203186788/.

13. Sean Hollister, "OnLive Lost: How the Paradise of Streaming Games Was Undone by One Man's Ego," The Verge, August 28, 2012, https://www.theverge.com/2012/8/28/3274739/onlive-report.

14. J. P. Mangalindan, "Cloud Gaming's History of False Starts and Promising Reboots," Polygon, October 15, 2020. https://www.polygon.com/features/2020/10/15/21499273/cloud-gaming-history-onlive-stadia-google.

15. Linda Poon, "There Are Far More Americans Without Broadband Access than Previously Thought," Bloomberg CityLab, February 19, 2020, https://www.bloomberg.com/news/articles/2020-02-19/where-the-u-s-underestimates-the-digital-divide.

16. Trey Paul, "5G Home Internet Might Be the Solution to Your Broadband Needs," CNet, January 5, 2020, https://www.cnet.com/home/internet/what-is-5g-home-internet.

17. Tom Daniels, "The Explosive Growth of Mobile Esports," *Esports Insider*, November 1, 2021, https://esportsinsider.com/2021/11/esj9-mobile-esports-growth.

18. Jason Schreier, "Blockchain in Gaming Is All the Rage for No Good Reason," Bloomberg, November 12, 2021, https://www.bloomberg.com/news/newsletters/2021-11-12/crypto-in-video-games-is-all-the-rage-but-why.

19. Andrew Hayward, "What Is Loot? The Surging Ethereum NFT Role-Playing Phenomenon," Decrypt, September 3, 2021, https://decrypt.co/80108/what-is-loot-ethereum-nft-role-playing-phenonemon.

20. Dean Takahashi, "Forte Raises $725M for Compliant Blockchain Gaming Platform," Venture Beat, November 12, 2021, https://venturebeat.com/2021/11/12/forte-raises-725m-for-compliant-blockchain-gaming-platform.

21. "Remembering the Wild West Era of Videogame Gold Farming," *Wired*, March 4, 2017, https://www.wired.com/2017/03/geeks-guide-gold-farming.

22. Alexis Ong, "Before Blockchains and NFTs, There Was the Real-Cash MMO Entropia Universe," *PC Gamer*, November 6, 2021, https://www.pcgamer.com/before-blockchain-and-nfts-there-was-the-real-cash-mmo-entropia-universe.

23. Taylor Hatmaker, "Discord Pushes Pause on Exploring Crypto and NFTs amidst User Backlash," *TechCrunch*, November 10, 2021, https://techcrunch.com/2021/11/10/discord-nfts-crypto-jason-citron.

24. Jonathan Stringfield, "For the Love of the Loot: Blockchain, The Metaverse and Gaming's Blind Spot," *TechCrunch*, September 16, 2021, https://techcrunch.com/2021/09/16/for-the-love-of-the-loot-blockchain-the-metaverse-and-gamings-blind-spot.

25. Gene Park, "Epic Games Believes the Internet Is Broken: This Is Their Blueprint to Fix It," *Washington Post*, September 28, 2021, https://www.washingtonpost.com/video-games/2021/09/28/epic-fortnite-metaverse-facebook.

26. Kyle Orland, "John Carmack Issues Some Words of Warning for Meta and Its Metaverse Plans," Ars Technica, October 29, 2021, https://arstechnica.com/gaming/2021/10/john-carmack-sounds-a-skeptical-note-over-metas-metaverse-plans.

27. Brian Fung, "Netflix: Fortnite Is a Bigger Rival than HBO," *Washington Post*, January 18, 2019, https://www.washingtonpost.com/technology/2019/01/18/netflix-fortnite-is-bigger-rival-than-hbo.

Chapter 11 Conclusion

1. Catie Keck, "Netflix's Gaming Push Could Be its Secret Sauce for Continued Domination," The Verge, November 9, 2021, https://www.theverge.com/22770244/netflix-gaming-app-launch-android-ios-future.

2. Henry Jenkins, *Convergence Culture: Where Old and New Media Collide* (New York: New York University Press, 2008), 3.

3. Ian Bogost, *How to Do Things with Videogames* (Minneapolis: University of Minnesota Press, 2011), 154.

4. Sherry Turkle, *Alone Together: Why We Expect More from Technology and Less from Each Other* (Perseus Books Group, 2011). Kindle Edition.

5. Ian Bogost, "The Metaverse Is Bad: It is Not a World in a Headset but a Fantasy of Power," *The Atlantic*, October 21, 2021, https://amp-theatlantic-com.cdn.ampproject.org/c/s/amp.theatlantic.com/amp/article/620449/.

Acknowledgments

This book, as a partial product of the circumstances of the COVID-19 global pandemic, is thus greatly indebted to those who were locked away with me for months on end: my wife, May; eldest son, Gabriel; and youngest son, Isaac. I am particularly grateful to both May and Gabriel for enthusiastically or begrudgingly (respectively) being my transcriptionists, research assistants, cheerleaders, or otherwise throughout the project. Thank you and I love you all.

I'm grateful to my father, Steve, for indulging my love of video games. Looks like some of those consoles were a decent investment! Though I'm still pretty miffed that you tossed a few of them (and some highly collectible PC game boxes), I love you all the same.

Thanks are due to a number of colleagues for having touch points on this project along the way. Thank you to Devora Rogers for putting the seed of "you should write a book" in my head, Kathe Sweeney for being an early believer and fan of the potential for this project, and Ryan Fox of Lyons & Salky Law for patiently walking me through the upfront business process. Thanks to Clement Xue for navigating some of the complexities around launching this project. Many thanks to Claire Nance and Joost Van Dreunen for graciously donating time to read, comment on, or sanity-check early drafts of this work. Additional thanks to Zoe Soon, Dan Holland, and Ross Siegel for reading through the manuscript before it was unleashed on the world, and Christina Verigan for ensuring it was (mostly) readable by that point.

Finally, thank you to the innumerable professionals who pour their love, creativity, and expertise into the art and science of creating video games. The impact of your work on billions of individuals like myself cannot be understated.

About the Author

Jonathan Stringfield is a research and marketing executive in technology and gaming, having spent almost 20 years at companies such as Facebook (Meta), Twitter, and Activision Blizzard. He is a regularly published contributor/speaker in technology on topics ranging from ad-tech to marketing science and consumer psychology. Jonathan holds a PhD in sociology, where his work concentrated on how users of new technology perform concepts such as personal identity. He has been published in academic journals on a diverse range of topics including new media, population displacement, and residential housing discrimination.

He is a resident of the New York City area with his wife May, sons Gabriel and Isaac, and dog Comet.

Index

233

Index